ollins

SNAP
REVISION
UNSEEN POETRY
AQA GCSE 9-1 English Literature

STEVE
EDDY

REVISE TRICKY
TOPICS IN A SNAP

Published by Collins
An imprint of HarperCollinsPublishers
1 London Bridge Street,
London, SE1 9GF

© HarperCollinsPublishers Limited 2018

9780008320119

First published 2018

10 9 8 7 6 5 4 3 2 1

Commissioning Editor: Gillian Bowman
Managing Editor: Craig Balfour
Author: Steve Eddy
Proofreader: Jill Laidlaw
Typesetting: Jouve
Cover designers: Kneath Associates and
  Sarah Duxbury
Production: Katharine Willard

ACKNOWLEDGEMENTS
p.5-6, 'Epitaph for a Wood-Turner' by Steve Eddy, reproduced by permission of Steve Eddy; p.12, 'A Small Girl Swinging' by George Szirtes, reproduced by permission of George Szirtes; p.14, 'Traffic' by Billy Collins, from The Rain in Portugal, reproduced by permission of Picador through PLSclear; p.15-16, 'A Cry from the Blue' by Shaun McCarthy, reproduced by permission of Shaun McCarthy; p.20-21, 'The Thief of Love' by Sheenagh Pugh, reproduced by permission of Seren Books; p.25, 'White Van Man' by Gillian Penrose, reproduced by permission of Gillian Penrose; p.28-29, 'Being Dead' by Paul Matthews, from This Naked Light (2018) published by Troubador Books, reproduced by permission of Paul Matthews, p.41, 'Bell Ringers' by Matthew Barton, from Vessel (2009), reproduced by permission of Matthew Barton; p.42, 'Campanologists' by Paul Groves, reproduced by permission of Seren Books; p.46, 'Nile Fingfisher' by Steve Eddy, reproduced by permission of Steve Eddy; p.47, 'Tench' by Steve Eddy, reproduced by permission of Steve Eddy; p.50-51, 'Fal Snow' by Matthew Barton, from Family Tree (2016), reproduced by permission of Matthew Barton and Shoestring Press; p.56, 'Long Ago' by Douglas Dunn, reproduced by permission of Faber & Faber Ltd; p.65, 'Night Ferry' by George Szirtes, reproduced by permission of George Szirtes; p.65-66, 'House on a Cliff' by Louis MacNeice, from Collected Poems, Faber & Faber Ltd.

The author and publisher are grateful to the copyright holders for permission to use quoted materials and images.

Every effort has been made to trace copyright holders and obtain their permission for the use of copyright material. The author and publisher will gladly receive information enabling them to rectify any error or omission in subsequent editions. All facts are correct at time of going to press.

Contents

How to Approach a Poem

Aspects of poetry

In your exam you will have to answer two questions on 'unseen poetry' – poems that you will probably not have read before. You will have had no chance to revise these. However, it *is* possible to learn, and practise, a method by which to analyse *any* poem.

This method consists of identifying the different elements outlined in this section, and commenting on whichever are most relevant to the poem. You will see that the elements can be memorised using the mnemonic sentence 'What Voice Forms Language?', where each word in the sentence is an element: 'What (is it about)', 'Voice', 'Forms' and 'Language'.

What is it about? Subject, theme and narrative

The first question to ask is – What is the poem about? (What is its subject?) The title may shed light on this – if it is more than just the first line repeated. It may tell you exactly what the poem is about, but it may not be that straightforward. Take the following poem by Anne Brontë:

Night

I love the silent hour of night,
      For blissful dreams may then arise,
Revealing to my charmèd sight
      What may not bless my waking eyes.

And then a voice may meet my ear,
      That death has silenced long ago;
And hope and rapture may appear
      Instead of solitude and woe.

Cold in the grave for years has lain
      The form it was my bliss to see;
And only dreams can bring again
      The darling of my heart to me.

is is, as the title suggests, partly about night, but it quickly becomes apparent that it is
hat happens at night that matters to the speaker: she dreams of someone she has loved
d lost. So, you could say that the poem is about dreams consoling the bereaved.

oking further into the ideas behind the poem, its **themes** could include death, longing
d imagination.

me poems are **narrative**: they tell a story. 'Night' tells no obvious story, but it does imply a
nple narrative: the speaker has lost a loved one; she is now lonely, but her grief is relieved
dreams.

oice, viewpoint, tone and mood

oice

poem's **voice** is the person or character whom we imagine speaking. We cannot assume
at this is simply the poet speaking directly to the reader, as sometimes the poet adopts a
rticular attitude for effect, so it is safer to write about 'the speaker'. For example:

> In 'Night' the speaker is consoled by dreams of a lost loved one.

me poems are written in character – adopting a **persona**, as in W. B. Yeats' poem
n Irish Airman Foresees his Death':

> I know that I shall meet my fate
>
> Somewhere among the clouds above;
>
> Those that I fight I do not hate,
>
> Those that I guard I do not love;
>
> …

ewpoint (perspective)

is largely refers to whether the poem is written in the first person, like the two poems
ove, the second person (addressing someone as 'you'), or the third person, like the short
itaph poem below:

Epitaph for a Wood-Turner

> He thought that he had been quite clever
>
> carving a career, making his mark.
>
> Turns out he was only ever
>
> whittling in the dark.

However, it is possible for a poet to write in the third person but still convey the attitude and character of an imagined speaker by writing in the kind of language they might use. For example, in 'Bob's Lane' (see page 26), Edward Thomas conveys a sense of the down-to-earth farmer's character by using straightforward language.

Tone and mood

These elements are closely related. **Tone** refers to how the poet addresses the reader – for example, in a conversational tone, or a bitter tone. In 'Epitaph for a wood-turner' the tone is darkly humorous, joking about the wood-turner 'whittling' (a **pun** on 'whistling') in the dark. This pun on a colloquial expression also makes the tone conversational.

Mood has more to do with a poem's overall emotional effect, though in a long poem the mood may change. The mood of Anne Brontë's 'Night' is one of sadness mixed with hope. Words like 'blissful', 'charmed' and 'rapture' contrast with 'solitude and woe', and 'Cold in the grave'.

Forms and structure

The **form** of a poem refers to its verse patterns and how it is divided into **stanzas**.

Verse patterns (prosody)

A poem could be in a **metre** – a pattern of lines consisting of a certain number of stressed and unstressed syllables. In both Anne Brontë's 'Night' and Yeats' 'An Irish Airman Foresees his Death', each line is composed of four pairs of syllables. Each pair consists of an unstressed syllable, followed by a stressed syllable:

> I <u>love</u> / the <u>si</u> / lent <u>hour</u> / of <u>night</u>
>
> I <u>know</u> / that <u>I</u> / shall <u>meet</u> / my <u>fate</u>

You will not earn many marks just by identifying the metre. However, good poets emphasise meaning by subtly varying the metre. For example, if you read 'Night' aloud, you should find that it moves along smoothly in a 'di-dum, di-dum ...' rhythm until you reach this line:

> Cold in the grave for years has lain

Sticking to the rhythm here would stress the word 'in', but it sounds more natural to stress 'Cold'. This, however, breaks the rhythm, drawing attention to the word and adding to its impact.

Form also includes **rhyme**, which is often used with metre to create pattern. The Brontë and Yeats poems have the same **rhyme scheme**. Line 1 rhymes with line 3; line 2 rhymes with line 4. Rhyme schemes are identified using letters: this would be called an *abab* rhyme scheme.

Again, you will not earn many marks just by pointing this out, but you will earn marks for explaining why it is appropriate, and how it is used to emphasise particular words. For example, Anne Brontë rhymes 'night' with 'sight', underlining the paradox that she 'sees' better in the dark.

Stanzas

A poem may be set out as one paragraph, or it may be split into stanzas. In a metrical poem, each stanza may be a basic unit of metre, with the metrical pattern being repeated in each stanza. Just as in prose, the poet may introduce a new idea in each new stanza, or a new development of the main theme.

Structure

This refers to the development of the poet's ideas. In a narrative poem, this may relate closely to the story. In a poem without a strong narrative, it may relate to the development of the poem's mood. Or the poet may describe an event or scene and then draw a conclusion from it.

Language

Poets choose words in order to achieve particular effects. For example, look again at the start of Yeats' poem:

> I know that I shall meet my fate
>
> Somewhere among the clouds above

He could have written, 'I know that I shall meet my death', but this would not have carried the same sense of his being resigned to the inevitable. Similarly, his use of 'among the clouds', rather than 'up in the sky', conveys a sense of mystery and uncertainty.

Connotations

The impact of individual words is influenced by what readers associate with them – their **connotations**. For example, Yeats uses the word 'clouds'. What ideas do you associate with clouds? This is up to you to explain. You might, for example, write:

> *The speaker's use of 'clouds' suggests a sense of mystery about how he will die.*

On the other hand, clouds can be associated with trouble, so there could be a deliberate **ambiguity** in Yeats' use of the word. Language can have layers of meaning, and alternative interpretations.

Imagery

Imagery uses comparison to create a word picture:

- **metaphors** speak of something as if it *is* something else, as in 'carving a career', which speaks of a career as if it were a piece of wood
- **similes** compare one thing with another more explicitly, using 'like', 'as' or 'than'
- **personification** is a special type of metaphor describing an abstract idea, such as love or time, as if it were a person or a god:

> But at my back I always hear
> Time's wingèd chariot hurrying near
> > Andrew Marvell, 'To his Coy Mistress'

These lines personify time as a charioteer.

Sound effects

The sounds of words also help to shape their meaning. The principal sound effects are:

- **alliteration** is the repetition of consonant (non-vowel) sounds at the beginnings of words or stressed syllables (e.g. 'carving a career, making his mark')
- **assonance** is the repetition of vowel sounds (e.g. 'carving ... mark')
- **onomatopoeia** is the use of words that sound like what they mean (e.g. 'buzz').

Summary

- Poems can be analysed by examining their key elements:
  - **What** they are about (subject, themes and narrative)
  - **Voice**, viewpoint, tone and mood
  - **Forms** (including metre, stanzas and rhyme) and structure
  - **Language** (including word choices, imagery and sound effects)
- These elements can be remembered using the mnemonic sentence 'What Voice Forms Language?'

Sample analysis

'Night' contrasts the 'love', 'bliss', 'hope' and 'rapture' that the speaker feels in her dreams with the awful sense of 'solitude and woe' that she feels when awake, because she has lost a loved one. The smoothly flowing **iambic** rhythm conveys her positive feelings while dreaming, but these are interrupted with shocking impact by the rhythmic change that comes with 'Cold in the grave', where sense requires the emphasis to be on 'Cold' rather than 'in'.

Questions

QUICK TEST
1. What is the difference between the subject of a poem and its themes?
2. What word is used for a set rhythmic pattern in a poem?
3. Which type of image uses 'like', 'as' or 'than'?

EXAM PRACTICE
Write a further paragraph commenting on the three-stanza structure of 'Night'.

What is it about? How Subject Relates to Theme

In most cases, the best thing to comment on first is what the poem seems to be about – its subject. With older poems, like the one below by William Wordsworth, this may be fairly obvious. Here are some typical types of subject:

• a character, dead or alive, and perhaps what they mean, or meant, to the poet

• an event – perhaps in the poet's life, or a historical event

• a place and its significance or atmosphere

• an animal and its nature.

Read the poem below and consider what it is about.

She Dwelt among the Untrodden Ways

She dwelt among the untrodden ways

Beside the springs of Dove,

A Maid whom there were none to praise

And very few to love:

A violet by a mossy stone

Half hidden from the eye!

—Fair as a star, when only one

Is shining in the sky.

She lived unknown, and few could know

When Lucy ceased to be;

But she is in her grave, and, oh,

The difference to me!

sking yourself questions

ou could probably work out that this poem is about 'Lucy', a girl or young woman known
the poet or his imagined speaker, that she has died, and that he misses her. The fact that
e has died makes it an **elegy**. To say more about the subject, and to explore its themes,
u would have to ask yourself some questions, and start to look for evidence in the poem
th which to answer them:

What is meant by 'untrodden ways', and how is it significant that she lived there?

How well-known was she? Was she a popular girl, adored by her many friends and
family members?

According to the speaker, what was Lucy like, and what images show this?

How does the speaker feel about her death, and how is this revealed?

u also have to look for what is *implied* – for example, by Lucy living in a remote place.

hemes

member that a poem's themes are the big ideas behind its apparent subject matter.
ese could include, for example, love, money, loss or childhood. Most good poems explore
emes rather than making a fixed statement with just one interpretation. Be aware,
o, that the language choices contribute to the themes, not just the story or apparent
eaning of the words.

, in this poem, some possible themes based on the questions above, are:

Innocence – Lucy lived 'among the untrodden ways', meaning far from towns or
villages, by a river whose name is a symbol of peace.

The natural goodness of someone brought up surrounded by nature. Wordsworth uses
nature imagery to describe her – the metaphor of a violet, a small, beautiful flower
that can grow in partial shade, and a simile comparing her with a star.

Virtue that goes unnoticed. Lucy 'lived unknown' and few were aware of her death.

Personal loss. The speaker's feelings are conveyed simply by the exclamation, 'oh/ The
difference to me!'.

oems with a less obvious subject

w read the modern poem on the next page. The subject has something in common
th Wordsworth's poem, and its language suggests childhood innocence. Yet what it is
ally about is open to interpretation. If you write about a poem like this, suggest possible
eanings or ideas; you are not expected to give a full explanation. However, you should
ck up your ideas with evidence from the text.

ad the poem a second time thinking about the annotations and how they might help
u to comment on its subject and themes.

A Small Girl Swinging

When first they pushed me
    I was very scared.
My tummy jiggled. I was
    Unprepared.

The second time was higher
    And my ears
Were cold with whisperings
    Of tiny fears.

The third time up was HIGH,
    My teeth on edge.
My heart leapt off the bedroom
    Window-ledge.

The fourth time, Oh, the fourth time
    It was mad.
My skirt flew off the world
    And I was glad.

No one's pushing now,
    My ears are ringing.
Who'll see across the park
    A small girl swinging?

Who'll hear across the park
    Her mother calling,
And everywhere her shadows
    Rising, falling?

George Szirtes

Who?

Childish language for fear.

Effect? Who or what is whispering?

Effect of capitals?

Excited or terrified?

Changed attitude; simple rhyme linking 'glad' to 'mad'.

What implied? Has she been abandoned?

Night approaching? Menace?

Summary

- Typical subjects are a character, an event or a significant place.
- To explore subject and themes, ask yourself questions and look for what is implied.
- Themes are the big ideas explored in a poem.
- You are not expected to give full, clear-cut explanations of poems.

Sample analysis

There is a sense of uncertainty throughout 'A Small Girl Swinging', especially in its narrative. At first sight it seems clear: stanza 1 is about the first time the girl was pushed, stanza 2 about the second time, and so on. However, the reader is left to wonder who the pronoun 'they' refers to, and later, how the girl continues to swing when 'No one's pushing'. Also, the narrative cannot be taken literally. The girl's heart cannot be on the 'bedroom window-ledge' if she is swinging, though the detail implies that she is thinking of being safe at home. Similarly, her skirt cannot literally fly 'off the world': this may be a childish expression of her excited sense of expanding horizons.

Questions

QUICK TEST

1. Which of these could *not* be a theme? Choose from: time, childhood, swinging, family, fear.
2. What should you always include if you suggest interpretations for what a poem is about?
3. What themes can you identify in 'She Dwelt among the Untrodden Ways'?
4. How would you describe the girl's feelings at the end of 'A Small Girl Swinging'?

EXAM PRACTICE

Write a further paragraph commenting on how the mood of 'A Small Girl Swinging' develops over the course of the poem.

'A Small Girl Swinging' in the previous section tells a story but does not describe realistic events. Nonetheless it implies a narrative of changing feelings, from childish fear, to exhilaration, to a sense of threat. Many narrative poems are more realistic than this. Ther are also narrative poems in which little happens; this may even be their point.

Narrative making a point

Some poems tell a story to make a point. Sometimes the poet tells a story and then comments on its meaning. In the poem below, the poet builds up details of what happen while he is in a traffic jam. How do the details create a sense of time passing?

Traffic

A child on a silver bicycle,

a young mother pushing a stroller,

and a runner who looked like he was

running to Patagonia

Patagonia – remote area on the southern tip of South America

have all passed my car, jammed

into a traffic jam on a summer weekend.

And now an elderly couple gradually

overtakes me as does a family of snails –

me stalled as if in a pit of tar

far from any beach and its salty air.

Why even Buddha has risen

from his habitual sitting

and is now walking serenely past my car,

Buddha – religious figure associated with calm and patien meditation.

holding his robes to his chest with one hand.

I watch him from the patch of shade

I have inched into as he begins to grow smaller

over my steering wheel then sits down again

up ahead, unfurling his palms

as if he were only a tiny figurine affixed to the dash.

Billy Collins

> ## Questions to consider

- At what point do the details become unrealistic, and what is the effect?
- What does the third stanza suggest about the poet's feelings, and where he might be going?
- Why does he introduce the Buddha?
- What is the effect of the final image?

ow poets comment on narrative

'Traffic' the poet makes no comment on his narrative. Some poems, however, tell a story
d then explore its meaning.

hereas 'Traffic' was about time passing slowly, with the speaker only able to observe the
idence, 'A Cry from the Blue', below, seems to be about a single moment in time, when
e speaker's lawnmower has stalled. The poet describes it, then considers its significance.

th poems are about time and place. In 'Traffic' the poet is stuck in one place; in 'A Cry
m the Blue' the speaker is intensely aware of his surroundings at a particular moment. In
both, narrative is linked to structure.

Cry from the Blue' begins with a narrative convention, setting the scene: time and
ather, then location.

Cry from the Blue

t was the middle afternoon,

ot and stinging, when suddenly

here was a cry from the blue, ◄─────────────── | Unexpected and urgent. |

rounded in no one place.

he field beyond the hedge was still,

othing slipped round the green corner

nd all points held the slight

urprise of inanimate objects ◄──────── | Personifies inanimate things – projecting own experience onto them? |

isturbed, in their essence, by humans.

Was it a call of warning

to a stealthy second that I was there,

crouched in the fuss of a stalled mower?

It was hard to say even if

human or creature voiced the syllable –

It was not god-like, certainly.

A simple cry from the blue, except

that field, lane and hedge were blank

as tape that awaits the press of sound;

a cry portentous as the tile

that falls in a dead calm, the pile

of books that crash in an empty room.

Shaun McCarthy

Annotations:
- Considers what it was.
- Person or moment in time?
- Not a religious experience?
- Waiting for something? (Tape was used for recording.)
- **Portentous** - full of ominous significance
- Unsettling – as if they have a life of their own.

Ironic narrative

Some poems imply an **irony** in the story – something seemingly inappropriate in a grimly comic way. In these poems it would be heavy-handed for the poet to explain the irony.

Read this poem by Thomas Hardy:

At the Railway Station, Upway

'There is not much that I can do,

     For I've no money that's quite my own!'

     Spoke up the pitying child –

A little boy with a violin

At the station before the train came in, –

'But I can play my fiddle to you,

And a nice one 'tis, and good in tone!'

The man in the handcuffs smiled;
The constable looked, and he smiled, too,
As the fiddle began to twang;
And the man in the handcuffs suddenly sang
With grimful glee:
This life so free
Is the thing for me!'
And the constable smiled, and said no word,
As if unconscious of what he heard;
And so they went on till the train came in –
The convict, and boy with the violin.

Questions to consider

- Why does the boy offer to play?
- What is implied by him owning a good violin, yet 'no money that's quite my own!'?
- What is ironic about the situation, and the boy's tune?
- What information does Hardy withhold till stanza 2, and why?

Summary

- Some poems use narrative to make a point.
- Not all narrative poems contain major events.
- Some poems tell a story, then explore its significance.
- Some narratives are ironic, usually leaving the reader to get the irony.

Sample analysis

'Traffic' is a narrative poem in which almost nothing happens – at least to the narrator. He is stuck in traffic, the simile of him being 'stalled as if in a pit of tar', suggesting both melting tarmac and his immobility. He begins with a realistic list of people who pass him, building up to the elderly couple, emphasising his lack of movement, but he begins to fantasise to make his point with the 'family of snails', and then the Buddha, a model of calm patience. This may suggest that the speaker is actually very frustrated, despite knowing that he should try to be like the Buddha.

Questions

QUICK TEST

1. Which of these are true statements?

   (a) Narrative poems are always realistic.

   (b) Some poems use narrative to make a point.

   (c) Poets sometimes comment on their own narrative.

2. To what feature of form is narrative often linked?

3. Why does the speaker in 'Traffic' describe the things that pass him?

EXAM PRACTICE

Write one or two paragraphs explaining what you think 'A Cry from the Blue' is about, and how its narrative contributes to this.

Voice, Viewpoint, Tone and Mood

Who is speaking?

Remember that you cannot assume that the observations, memories and views in the poem are simply those of the poet. This is most obvious in poems where the poet adopts a persona, taking on the perspective of another person, real or imagined.

The poet may be trying to give readers an insight into the kind of person whose voice is presented. If so, you will need to ask yourself what this person is like, and how their outlook would be typical of a particular class of person – such as an ordinary soldier. Consider:

- their views
- how they describe themselves
- what kind of language they use.

Here is the whole of the Yeats poem introduced on page 7. It was written in 1918.

An Irish Airman Foresees his Death

I know that I shall meet my fate
Somewhere among the clouds above;
Those that I fight I do not hate,
Those that I guard I do not love;
My country is Kiltartan Cross,
My countrymen Kiltartan's poor,
No likely end could bring them loss
Or leave them happier than before.
Nor law, nor duty bade me fight,
Nor public men, nor cheering crowds,
A lonely impulse of delight
Drove to this tumult in the clouds;
I balanced all, brought all to mind,
The years to come seemed waste of breath,
A waste of breath the years behind
In balance with this life, this death.

- What does the airman's attitude towards death seem to be in the first two lines?
- How is this developed in the final four lines?
- Does he seem patriotic? What evidence is there?
- What people does he identify with, and how does the language emphasise this?
- What attitude to the outcome of war does he express, and how?
- What seems to be his reason for risking his life as a pilot?

Persona or metaphor?

In some poems it is obvious that a persona is being used, but it may be less obvious whether it is meant to represent a class of person, such as soldiers in general, or the poor, or whether it represents an idea or a metaphor.

Read the following poem by Sheenagh Pugh once, then again considering the annotation Try to form a picture of the imagined speaker, their desires, their moral code, and what they represent.

The Thief of Love

I will come like a thief if I have to,

soft-footed. I won't force an entry,

just find one,

some sash with a gap. I'll slip

a fingertip in, ease it open

while you're asleep.

You'll be out when I feel your cool sheets ◄──── Very intimate. Effect?

on my skin, when I stroll through your rooms ◄──── What is implied by this word choice?

handling, enjoying.

I'll access your email, your passwords,

click on your history, trace you

through cyberspace.

)id you think I would come to the door

──► **Rhetorical question**. Effect?

s honest folk do; play fair?

,ove has no pride,

o honour; it takes what it's given

nd what it can get. It begs ◄──────── Is this person a lover?
A metaphor for love itself?

vithout shame; why not this?

nd I am each chancer, levanter ◄──────── Exotic term for someone who
flees leaving unpaid debts.

nd picklock who gives his heart freely

o what's out of reach, ◄──────── The key to the persona?

ar above, safely owned, and schemes how

o coax it to hand, one way

r another.

orking out the persona

member that there may not be a straightforward explanation. Analysing a poem is not
t a piece of difficult detective work! How would you characterise the approach of the
eaker in this poem? For example, which words below might you use?

bold	assertive	indirect	surreptitious	ethical
unscrupulous	menacing	playful	devious	stealthy

may be that you think two or three of these words are appropriate, perhaps relating to
'ferent points in the poem. The next stage of your analysis would be to find evidence in
e form of short quotations to back up your description. You should try to focus on the
tual language used, not just the ideas conveyed. For example, you might say:

> The **sibilance** of words like 'soft', 'sash', 'sleep' 'skin' and even 'cyberspace'
> emphasises the stealthy, insidious approach of this persona to someone else's
> private world.

Interpretations

Having worked out the character of the persona, you can consider possible interpretation
In the case of 'The Thief of Love', the title is open to interpretation too. It could refer to:

- love itself being a thief
- someone destroying love
- someone stealing a kind of intimacy – such as a stalker.

Which idea do you find more convincing, and why? What lines from the poem back up your view?

Summary

- A character through whom a poet 'speaks' a poem is called a persona.
- A persona could represent a class of person, such as a member of the Irish rural poor.
- A persona could be a metaphor.
- The persona's language is an important clue to their character and purpose.

Sample analysis

In 'The Thief of Love' the poet presents a mysterious and even sinister persona. The use of the first person and the technique of addressing the person whose privacy is invaded as 'you' creates an uncomfortable sense of intimacy, particularly in 'I feel your cool sheets/ on my skin', and the sibilant 's' sounds of 'skin' and 'stroll' create a sense of this persona stealthily infiltrating someone's life, perhaps like a stalker. The mention of 'cyberspace' adds to this sound effect, but is also a real threat.

Questions

QUICK TEST
1. How does Yeats inform us about his airman's social background?
2. To whom is 'The Thief of Love' addressed, and why is this uncomfortable for the reader?
3. In which line does 'The Thief of Love' broaden the persona's identity from an individual to something more universal?

EXAM PRACTICE
Write a paragraph about the character of Yeats' airman and how the poem's details and language reveal it.

Viewpoint, or Perspective

ewpoint' here denotes the point of view from which the poem is written. This could be:

first person, like a 'persona poem'

second person, addressing someone, or the reader, as 'you'

third person, using 'he', 'she' or 'it'.

:ould also be in the present or past tense. Present tense normally creates a sense of
mediacy. The past tense would normally describe past events, for example the life of
neone no longer living.

rst-person poems

some first-person poems the poet is describing their own thoughts, feelings and
periences, though it is safer to write about 'the speaker', because you cannot be sure
s is the case.

ntrast the persona poems in the previous section with the following poem, in which it is
ely that the poet is simply expressing her own feelings:

A Birthday

My heart is like a singing bird ◄——— | Series of present-tense similes expressing joy.

    Whose nest is in a water'd shoot;

My heart is like an apple-tree

    Whose boughs are bent with thickset fruit;

My heart is like a rainbow shell

    That paddles in a halcyon sea; | **Halcyon** – idyllically tranquil, warm and happy

My heart is gladder than all these

    Because my love is come to me. | Series of commands, as if she is a queen – must be how she feels.

Raise me a dais of silk and down; ◄———

    Hang it with vair and purple dyes; | **Vair** – squirrel fur – a luxury

Carve it in doves and pomegranates,

    And peacocks with a hundred eyes;

Work it in gold and silver grapes,

    In leaves and silver fleurs-de-lys;

Because the birthday of my life

    Is come, my love is come to me.

            Christina Rossetti

> **Fleurs-de-lys** – a stylised three-headed lily used in royal coats of arm

> More than just a birthday?

> A human lover, or is this a religious poem?

Second-person poems

A first-person poem could address a lover or friend, but it is also possible for a poem to b entirely in the second person, without using the 'I' of the speaker or poet. For example, t poet may wish to commemorate someone who has died.

More often the poet refers to their relationship with the person addressed. If this is the case, try to work out from the poem's language how the poet is presenting the relationship, as in the beginning of D. H. Lawrence's poem 'Last Words to Miriam':

> Yours is the sullen sorrow,
>
>   The disgrace is also mine;
>
> Your love was intense and thorough,
>
> Mine was the love of a growing flower
>
>   For the sunshine.

The negative 'sullen sorrow' and 'disgrace' suggest that the relationship has failed, although the fresh, natural flower metaphor shows that it was once healthy, even if perhaps Lawrence sees himself as benefitting more from it than the woman he is addressing. He also uses tense to contrast the sad present with the happier past.

Third-person poems

This is a common type of poem. You may, for example, be presented with a poem describing a character. Just as in a novel, the character could be revealed in several ways, including appearance, actions, speech and direct description.

White Van Man

He had a convenience store
on the dashboard:

a half-eaten sandwich in its box
two chocolate snack wrappers
one full fizzy drink can, one crushed
yesterday's Mirror open at the football;
sturdy gloves (large size)
rather thin on the right thumb;
aviator-style sun glasses hooked on the steering wheel
one lens cracked.

On the passenger seat:
a hard hat and hi-viz jacket
once bright yellow
draped over a grubby clipboard, biro attached.

On the floor:
a confetti of boiled sweet wrappers
obscuring a half-bottle of water
parked under the accelerator.

No Tools Are Kept In This Van Overnight
said a sticker on the rear door;
no brains either had been added in the grime.

What nobody could see until after the accident
was a fusty sleeping bag in the back
an electric razor
a dog-eared photo of his kids.

Gillian Penrose

Ask yourself

- What is implied by the opening stanza, including its tense?
- What do the details tell you about the man's lifestyle?
- What does the association of 'crushed', 'cracked', 'grubby' and 'grime' with this man imply?
- What context for this account do you imagine? Why?

Appearance, description and actions

The poem below conveys someone's character by describing his appearance, what he appreciated, and what he did.

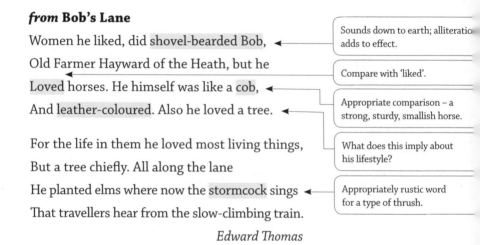

from Bob's Lane

Women he liked, did shovel-bearded Bob, ◄———— Sounds down to earth; alliteratio adds to effect.

Old Farmer Hayward of the Heath, but he

►———— Compare with 'liked'.

Loved horses. He himself was like a cob, ◄————

And leather-coloured. Also he loved a tree. ◄————

Appropriate comparison – a strong, sturdy, smallish horse.

For the life in them he loved most living things,

But a tree chiefly. All along the lane

What does this imply about his lifestyle?

He planted elms where now the stormcock sings ◄————

Appropriately rustic word for a type of thrush.

That travellers hear from the slow-climbing train.

Edward Thomas

Summary

Poems can be in the first, second or third person.

A first-person poem might describe the speaker's feelings and thoughts.

A third-person poem might convey character through the details of someone's life, appearance, likes and loves, and actions.

Word choices may reflect the character.

Sample analysis

n 'White Van Man' a sense of character is built up by physical details. The man bought is daily requirements in convenience stores. He may have been interrupted in eating is sandwich – perhaps by the accident in the final stanza. He seems to have done a argely physical job with an element of danger, shown by the hard hat, hi-viz jacket nd worn gloves. The mess of wrappers implies that he only had himself to please, the 'usty' sleeping bag that his van was his home, perhaps due to divorce. He must have iewed the 'dog-eared' photo frequently, missing his children. The words 'crushed', cracked', 'grubby' and 'grime' imply a broken and unloved life, the sadness of which is eepened by the man's anonymity.

Questions

UICK TEST

.   What three pronouns denote the third person?

.   How do the two stanzas of 'A Birthday' contrast with each other?

.   What is the likely effect of a poem using the present tense?

.   How does the phrase 'shovel-bearded Bob' convey character?

XAM PRACTICE

Vrite a paragraph about the character of Edward Thomas's 'Bob' and how the poem's etails and language reveal it.

Tone and Mood

These terms are sometimes used loosely to mean the same thing, and sometimes they are very closely related. However, it is more accurate to define them as follows:

- **tone** is the manner in which the poet addresses the reader, or someone to whom the poem is directed – such as conversationally, intimately, formally or informally
- **mood** is the overall emotional effect of the poem – though the mood can also change as the poem develops, especially in a long poem.

Tone

Read the following poem, addressed to someone who has died. Consider the way in which the speaker addresses the person who is the subject of the poem, the kind of language used, and the way it uses repetition of the opening line.

Being Dead

For Patricia T

It doesn't really suit you, being dead.
You were the world's bright-eyed receptionist.
You held the important numbers in your head.

> A literal receptionist?
> A receiver of the world? Both?

I never thought to view you in such a bed
Laid out in this quiet place of rest.
It doesn't quite become you, being dead.

> Varies wording.

A bird's brilliance filled the life you led.
I'm glad you've kept the bangles at your wrist
As all the jingling numbers leave your head.

> Sound effect, like phone ringing.

The tittle-tattle now, it must be said,

> Gossip – but what kind?

Without your talent lacks its former zest.

> Formal tone – used ironically?

It isn't quite your style, this being dead.

o spry you were. For counsel now instead

Formal word for 'advice'.

Ve'll make enquiry at the wind's front desk.

t really doesn't suit you being dead.

ou go with all our numbers round your head.

Paul Matthews

k yourself

Is the poem flippant, given the subject, or just lively?

What is the speaker's attitude to the person addressed?

How is polite or formal language used for effect?

How does the poet give a sense of what the person was like?

What is the rhyme scheme, and how does it affect the tone?

ood

ery poem has a mood, but a poem with a strong emotional content will have a more vious mood. The poem below contains great emotional power. It could be compared th 'Being Dead' in that it is addressed to someone deceased, but as if they are still ve. Both poets, in very different ways, seem to struggle with the fact that the woman dressed is no longer alive. Read 'The Voice' aloud to get its full effect.

he Voice

Voman much missed, how you call to me, call to me,

aying that now you are not as you were

Vhen you had changed from the one who was all to me,

Sounds as if something went wrong *before* she died.

ut as at first, when our day was fair.

an it be you that I hear? Let me view you, then,

Hardly dares believe it.

tanding as when I drew near to the town

Vhere you would wait for me: yes, as I knew you then,

ven to the original air-blue gown!

Or is it only the breeze, in its listlessness

Travelling across the wet mead to me here, ← Back to reality of wintry meadow.

You being ever dissolved to wan wistlessness, ← *Wan* is pale; *wistlessness* probably means 'unknowing'.

Heard no more again far or near?

Thus I; faltering forward, ← Rhythm changes – effect?

Leaves around me falling,

Wind oozing thin through the thorn from norward,

And the woman calling.

Thomas Hardy

Ask yourself

- What is the effect of the strong rhythm, and its change in the final stanza?
- The mood of this poem is never happy, but how does it change?
- How does sensory appeal affect the mood of the poem? Look especially at stanzas 2 and 4.
- How would you sum up the mood at the end, and what especially creates this?

Summary

- Tone is related to the poet's style of address; mood more to emotional effect.
- Rhyme and ironically formal language can influence tone.
- Strongly emotional poems have a more obvious mood.
- Mood can develop as a poem progresses.

Sample analysis

n 'Being Dead', the tone is surprisingly light, given the subject. The speaker addresses he deceased subject directly, using **litotes** (understatement) ironically, as if being dead vere something that someone could wear, like a dress. He seems to do this to convey ow alive the woman always seemed, emphasised by the onomatopoeic 'bangles' and ingling'. The playful and slightly mischievous 'tittle-tattle' adds the idea that the woman vas very engaged in other people's lives, while the fact that it now 'lacks its former zest' playfully formal, also suggesting her playfulness.

Questions

UICK TEST
. What is the difference between tone and mood?
. What kind of poems have a more obvious mood?
. What techniques make 'Being Dead' seem light-hearted?
. What techniques particularly change the mood in 'The Voice'?

XAM PRACTICE
Vrite a paragraph explaining how sensory details and rhythm develop the mood in 'he Voice'.

Forms

Rhythm and metre (prosody)

All poems have rhythms, but not all use a metre. A rhythm is simply a pattern created by the natural occurrence of stressed and unstressed syllables in speech – because we do not speak like robots. For example:

> I <u>put</u> my <u>hat</u> up<u>on</u> my <u>head</u>
>
> And <u>walked</u> in<u>to</u> the <u>Strand</u>
>
> And there I met another man
>
> Whose hat was in his hand.

> *Samuel Johnson*

The stressed syllables are underlined in the first two lines. Where would they come in the remaining two? Tap out the rhythm while speaking the lines aloud. Try speaking a line with the opposite emphasis: it will sound very odd:

> <u>I</u> put <u>my</u> hat u<u>pon</u> <u>my</u> head

Types of rhythm

When you write about rhythm, it is important to analyse how it helps to create the meaning and impact of the poem, and how the poet varies it for effect. Not many good poems are entirely in one rhythm. Bear in mind, too, that although it is helpful to know the technical terms in this section, the really important thing is to notice the rhythms and comment on their effects.

Iambic rhythm

The commonest rhythm is **iambic**. This uses a metrical **foot** of two syllables – an unstressed followed by a stressed. In the iambic rhythm each foot is an **iamb**.

Shakespeare wrote most of his verse in iambic rhythm, as in:

> My <u>mi</u>stress' <u>eyes</u> are <u>no</u>thing <u>like</u> the <u>sun</u>

Other rhythms are explored below.

Trochaic rhythm

A **trochee** is a foot of two syllables, one stressed and one unstressed – the opposite of an iamb. It creates a forceful, pounding rhythm, as in Henry Longfellow's 'The Song of Hiawatha', which imitates Native American drumming:

By the shore of Gitche Gumee,

By the shining Big-Sea-Water,

At the doorway of his wigwam,

In the pleasant Summer morning,

Hiawatha stood and waited.

ems written entirely in trochees are rare, and those that employ trochaic lines normally it the final syllable, as in John Donne's 'Song: Go and Catch a Falling Star':

Go and catch a falling star,

       Get with child a mandrake root,

Tell me where all past years are,

       Or who cleft the devil's foot,

Teach me to hear mermaids singing,

Or to keep off envy's stinging,

       And find

       What wind

Serves to advance an honest mind.

actylic rhythm

dactyl is a foot of three syllables, one stressed and two unstressed. It tends to create a gging, solemn effect, though in Tennyson's 'The Charge of the Light Brigade' it also nds like cantering horses' hooves:

Half a league, half a league,

Half a league onward,

All in the valley of Death

       Rode the six hundred.

apaestic rhythm

anapaest is a rhythmic foot of three syllables, two unstressed and one stressed.
reates a rolling, galloping or charging effect, as in Byron's 'The Destruction of nacherib':

> The Assyrian came <u>down</u> like the <u>wolf</u> on the <u>fold</u>,
>
> And his cohorts were gleaming in purple and gold ...

However, the anapaest is also used in comic verse, notably the **limerick**:

> There <u>was</u> a young <u>man</u> from Dun<u>dee</u> ...

Metre

The metre of a poem is its rhythmic pattern, including the types and numbers of **feet** it ha in a line. The name of a metre combines its rhythm with the number of its feet. Metre is often reinforced by rhyme, with a rhyme coming at the end of some, or all, lines. It can al be made to seem less rigid, and more natural, by the use of **enjambment** continuing the sense from one line to the next.

Pentameter

The commonest English verse form is **iambic pentameter**. Remember that an 'iamb' is a foot of one unstressed and one stressed syllable: *di-dum*. The prefix *pent*, from Greek, means 'five'. So, a line of iambic pentameter has five iambic feet.

The **blank verse** mostly used by Shakespeare in his plays is unrhymed (blank) iambic pentameter.

Tetrameter

Tetrameter refers to a line of four feet. Samuel Johnson's rhyme, above, is in **iambic tetramet**

> I <u>put</u> / my <u>hat</u> / up<u>on</u> / my <u>head</u>

Trimeter

Trimeter refers to a line of three feet. It is more unusual, is used in nursery rhymes:

> Cock-a /-doodle/ -do
>
> The dame / has lost / her shoe.

Some lines in 'A Small Girl Swinging' are in trimeter:

> My skirt flew off the world

These help to give the poem its childlike quality.

Traditional metres

Some traditional poetic forms employ set metres and rhyme schemes. You do not need to learn these, but it is worth knowing about one example, the **ballad**. A ballad tells a story, and most are quite long, so you are unlikely to be given one in the exam. However, you may be given a poem in **ballad metre**.

llad metre is in stanzas of four lines (**quatrains**). Lines 1 and 3 are in tetrameter (four •t); lines 2 and 4 are in trimeter (three feet). Lines 2 and 4 usually rhyme.

example is Coleridge's 'The Rime of the Ancient Mariner', which tells the story of a or losing all his shipmates:

> Day after day, day after day,
> We stuck, nor breath nor motion;
> As idle as a painted ship
> Upon a painted ocean.

Summary

Rhythm is the pattern of stressed and unstressed syllables.

Different rhythms have different effects.

A metre is a pattern of rhythm and number of metrical feet.

Comment on how rhythm creates meaning and impact.

Sample analysis

ohn Donne uses a powerful trochaic rhythm that sounds like a magic spell being nanted. This fits with the poem presenting a series of imperatives: 'Go ... Get ... Tell ... each'. The impact of each fresh command is accentuated by these monosyllabic words. e gives a list of impossible supernatural challenges. However, the point of the first anza is that it is equally hard to avoid the effects of envy, or to find how to benefit om honesty. The metre suddenly changes, slowing the reader down to consider this. ne effect is increased by the rhyming triplet at the end.

Questions

UICK TEST

What is the commonest rhythm in English poetry?

What is 'pentameter'?

What is a metrical 'foot'?

How do poets use rhythm to create or reflect their meaning?

KAM PRACTICE

eread 'A Small Girl Swinging' (page 12) Write a paragraph analysing how it creates eaning and character by its use of rhythm.

Structure

To comment on rhythm or language you 'zoom in' and look at the details of a poem; to comment on structure you have to 'zoom out' and get an overview. This is like looking at a landscape instead of at one flower!

To analyse the structure of a poem, consider:

- Does the poem tell a story?
- Does it develop ideas over the course of the poem?
- Does the mood change, or intensify?
- Does the rhythm change the pace – as in the last stanza of 'The Voice' (pages 29–30)?
- Do stanzas (see below) break the poem up into stages of development?

Stanzas

A stanza is a separate section of verse. Sometimes the word 'verse' is used for this division but 'stanza' avoids confusion. The previous section of this guide explained how a poetic metre repeats itself in each stanza. However, some poems that do not use a metre still use stanzas. Sometimes the stanzas reflect the structure, for example by introducing new idea or thematic developments.

In the following poem, stanzas relate to the metre and structure the development of the poet's ideas.

Piano

Softly, in the dusk, a woman is singing to me;
Taking me back down the vista of years, till I see
A child sitting under the piano, in the boom of the tingling strings
And pressing the small, poised feet of a mother who smiles as she sings.

In spite of myself, the insidious mastery of song
Betrays me back, till the heart of me weeps to belong
To the old Sunday evenings at home, with winter outside
And hymns in the cosy parlour, the tinkling piano our guide.

So now it is vain for the singer to burst into clamour
With the great black piano appassionato. The glamour
Of childish days is upon me, my manhood is cast
Down in the flood of remembrance, I weep like a child for the past.

D. H. Lawrence

Like many poems, this tells a story. It is in three stages:

Stanza 1 sets the scene. The speaker is listening to a woman singing, and it makes him remember himself as a child sitting under the piano while his mother plays and sings.

Stanza 2 describes how the seductive power of music ('insidious mastery of song') returns him emotionally to the 'cosy parlour' of his childhood, with his mother at the piano.

Stanza 3 returns to the present, saying it is pointless ('vain') for the woman to sing, accompanied by the grand piano. He is not really listening, because he is swept away by the alluring magical power ('glamour') of his memories, so that he weeps for his lost childhood.

How detail reflects structure

Now read Lawrence's poem again to see how its language fits its development.

Softly, in the dusk, a woman is singing to me; ◄ — Atmospheric narrative scene-setting.

Taking me back down the vista of years, till I see ◄ — Going 'back' in time.

A child sitting under the piano in the boom of the ◄ — Pictures his childhood self.
    tingling strings

And pressing the small, poised feet of a mother — Seductive sibilant 's' sounds and powerful anapaestic rhythm reflect how he is swept 'back', betrayed by emotion.
    who smiles as she sings.

In spite of myself, the insidious mastery of song ◄

Betrays me back, till the heart of me weeps to belong — Vision of secure family home grows in strength.

To the old Sunday evenings at home, with
    winter outside

And hymns in the cosy parlour, the tinkling piano ◄ — Returns to present moment.
    our guide.

So now it is vain for the singer to burst into clamour ◄ — Loud and overbearing compared with mother – comparing past and present; rhythm speeds up approaching climax.

With the great black piano appassionato. ◄ — Contrasts with childhood piano (probably smaller); *appassionato* classical music term for 'with passion' – contrasts with mother's homely music.
    The glamour

Of childish days is upon me, my manhood is cast

Down in the flood of remembrance, I weep like — Relates to tears; brings poem to a climax.
    a child for the past. ◄ — Unites present and past.

The sonnet

Sometimes the structure is linked to a particular verse form, so look out for this in the exam

The most obvious verse form relating to structure is the **sonnet**. Sonnets are rhyming poems of fourteen lines of iambic pentameter. In the **Petrarchan sonnet**, the first eight lines (the **octave**) put forward an idea, while the final six (the **sestet**) develop it in a new direction, often bringing it to a resolution. The **Shakespearean sonnet** has a different rhyme scheme, and usually saves the change of direction for a final rhyming **couplet**.

The sonnet below is about the beauty of nature, and particularly its sounds. But see how first eight lines (the octave) and remaining six lines (the sestet) describe different aspects this theme.

On the Grasshopper and Cricket

The poetry of earth is never dead:

When all the birds are faint with the hot sun,

And hide in cooling trees, a voice will run

From hedge to hedge about the new-mown mead;

> **Mead** – meadow, field

That is the Grasshopper's – he takes the lead

In summer luxury, he has never done

With his delights; for when tired out with fun

He rests at ease beneath some pleasant weed.

The poetry of earth is ceasing never:

On a lone winter evening, when the frost

Has wrought a silence, from the stove there shrills

The Cricket's song, in warmth increasing ever,

And seems to one in drowsiness half lost,

The Grasshopper's among some grassy hills.

> **Cricket** – insect like a grasshopper that once lived near stoves in old houses

John Keats

What is the theme of the octave?

How does Keats develop this in the sestet?

How does Keats use repetition to link the two parts of the poem, and to what effect?

What mistake does Keats describe a sleepy listener making, and how does this link the octave and sestet?

Summary

A stanza is a verse paragraph.

In metrical poems, the metre repeats itself in each stanza.

Stanzas can reflect structure.

Language and rhythm reflect structure.

In typical sonnets, the octave sets out an idea, and the sestet develops it.

Sample analysis

'iano' tells a short story that moves from present to past, and then back to the resent. Stanza 1 creates an atmospheric narrative setting, with the sibilant 'Softly, in ne dusk', and reveals that the poet, or speaker, is at a concert listening to a piano and ocalist. The sound takes him gradually back to his childhood as if his eyes travel over landscape 'vista' to somewhere in the far distance. The second stanza remains largely the past, as the 'cosy' picture of the secure family home intensifies, even though it is ne present 'mastery of song' that takes him there. The final stanza shocks the reader ack into the present with the word 'clamour', comparing unfavourably with the hildhood memories. The poem reaches a climax in the metaphorical 'flood' of memory, oncluding with the union of past and present as the speaker weeps for the past.

Questions

UICK TEST

. How do stanzas often relate to metre?

. What simple and common structure does 'Piano' follow?

. What tense is 'Piano' written in, and how might this reinforce its main theme?

. What are the names for the two parts of a traditional sonnet?

XAM PRACTICE

/rite a paragraph analysing the effect of structure in 'On the Grasshopper and Cricket'.

Word choice, connotation and symbolism

Every word of a poem has been chosen by the poet. You will never appreciate a poem full or analyse it successfully if you just explore its ideas or its story, and not its language.

Tone

This guide has already explored tone in terms of the poet's way of addressing the reader. can also be applied to individual words, especially to their level of formality. In 'A Small G Swinging' (page 12) the tone of 'My tummy jiggled' is childishly informal. A more formal, adult version would be 'My stomach churned,' but this lacks the effect of childish naivety.

Similarly, in 'Being Dead' (pages 28–29) 'tittle-tattle' is informal and suggests slightly improper but largely harmless gossip. The word 'gossip' would lack the same hint of mischievous impropriety.

Another example of tone is found in 'Piano' (pages 37–38). Lawrence writes: 'it is vain for the singer to burst into clamour'. 'Vain' here means 'useless' or 'pointless', but there is a hint of the more modern meaning of 'self-admiring'. This fits with the critical tone of 'bu into clamour'. To 'burst' into song sounds sudden and insensitive; worse, 'clamour' indica a loud, annoying, attention-seeking noise, like dogs barking.

Connotations

A **connotation** is an association. We all associate different words with different things. W might, for example, associate 'snow' with cold, Christmas, purity, fun or avalanches. Poet choose words for their connotations as well as for their sound. Often, they intend more than one connotation.

Words in poems, then, frequently have layers of meaning, rather than a single straightforwa one. For example, what do you associate with the word 'glamour'? You could write the word on a sheet of paper and add your ideas in a spider diagram or 'thought shower' around it.

When, in 'Piano', Lawrence writes 'The glamour/ Of childish days is upon me', 'glamour' i surprising choice. He implies that he has been overpowered. The word suggests a powerf but untrustworthy attraction. This relates to an old meaning of the word – 'enchantment Even now someone might write about 'the tempting glamour of the fashion world', implying that it is less appealing beneath the glossy surface.

In Lawrence's poem, the negative connotations of 'glamour' link to the earlier lines: 'In spite of myself, the insidious mastery of song/ Betrays me back ...'. 'Insidious' suggests damage that happens gradually, unnoticed, caused by cunning. 'Betrays' has even more obviously negative connotations.

We could therefore say that 'glamour' is ambiguous: it has more than one meaning. Furthermore, it expresses the speaker's mixed feelings about being overcome by possibly unreliable memories.

Symbolism

Symbolism refers to things mentioned in a poem that somehow represent broader ideas. In the two poems that follow, two modern poets write about church bell-ringing and draw out their ideas about what the activity signifies. So, in each poem the same central symbol is used in different ways.

Bell ringers (campanologists) stand in a circle and pull ropes connected to the bells in a tower above. The bell's swinging pulls the rope back up. The ringers pull in a sequence to create a repeated tune.

Bell Ringers

This is the factory floor
where all the clanging parts
are hammered, welded into one:

> Onomatopoeia; 'parts' as in bell mechanism, musical parts, and ringers?

a circle of workers lift
arms to pull down molten heaven
on their heads and thresh it

> Farmers thresh corn to get the grain.

for all it's worth in a great collapse
of scaffolding, then feel the answering
tug of grace that draws them up

> Sounds like falling scaffolding? Parts linked like scaffolding?

the living cord to a deep
well above: the engine room
of a heart that's hauling a whole

> Paradoxical image.

invisible world down to make it
matter, sending at each stroke a rush
of light into the perfect, ringing

> Pun: 'stuff' (noun); 'count for something' (verb).

bowl each single presence of mind
makes by being separate together.

> Ringers concentrate individually to make joint music.

Matthew Barton

Campanologists

It is as if they are milking the idea
of angels, trying to draw down heaven
through the tower with the strain
they are creating, cancelling fear

of the grave's silence by railing against
a mute God via the bells' din,
the raucous tintinnabulation
that airs their complaints

and grievances for over an hour
while they stand in a circle, facing
each other, wordlessly embracing
thick ropes which transmit power

to unseen clappers as twilight falls
around the church like a soft mist
completely at odds with each red fist
and the manic rhythm, the crazed pulse

of complaint and entreaty, ringing the changes
yet still getting nowhere other than bed
– that linen tomb – when all is said
and done: the patterns, the exchanges.

Paul Groves

> Like cows – effect?

> Pun: effort and music.

> God does not speak to them.

> Onomatopoeia suggests loud ringing.

> Atmospheric contrast – suggests death?

> Pun: at the end of the day; but also, the dead can no longer speak or act.

What positive language in 'Bell Ringers' suggests what meaning the poet sees in bell-ringing?

What does 'Campanologists' suggest is the bell-ringers' motivation, and how is this shown?

What significant imagery does each poem use, and how does it create meaning?

What examples can you find of each poet choosing particular words for effect?

Summary

- Words have tone – especially level of formality, and how positive or negative they are.
- Poets choose words for their connotations – what people associate with them.
- Words can be ambiguous, giving poems layers of meaning.
- Symbolism refers to things that are used to represent broader ideas.

Sample analysis

Bell Ringers' presents the bell-ringing room as a place of work, a 'factory floor', implying that the ringers are working together to make a product. The harsh onomatopoeia of 'clanging parts', with the hard, industrial verbs 'hammered' and welded', suggest that this is hard work, even though the ringers pull down 'molten heaven'. The word 'parts' could refer to mechanisms, or musical parts, or the ringers themselves: they make music but they are also forging a relationship together.

Questions

QUICK TEST
. What is the tone of 'My tummy jiggled'?
. How does Lawrence use possible connotations of 'glamour'?
. What is symbolism in a poem?
. What does the 'factory floor' metaphor imply in 'Bell Ringers'?

XAM PRACTICE
Write a paragraph analysing the poet's word choices and ambiguities in Campanologists'.

Imagery

Imagery uses comparisons to create word pictures:

- metaphors speak of something as if it *is* something else, as in the bell room in 'Bell Ringers' being a 'factory floor'
- similes compare one thing with another using 'like', 'as' or 'than', as in the 'Campanologists', where they are pulling on ropes 'as if they are milking the idea/ of angels'
- personification describes an abstract idea as if it were a person or a god, as when Lawrence speaks of 'the insidious mastery of song', making music sound like a crafty person overpowering him.

Appropriate imagery

All types of image have to be appropriate to be effective. What makes this metaphor fro 'Bell Ringers' effective?

> This is the factory floor
>
> where all the clanging parts
>
> are hammered, welded into one ...

The poet is picturing an old-fashioned factory where workers noisily hammer and weld metal, working together to produce parts that will fit together. So, there are several similarities:

- noise
- metalwork
- a shared goal.

At the same time, for a metaphor to be effective, there must be differences too, to make the similarities surprising. It would be less effective to describe the bell-ringers as 'a chamber orchestra' because that is too close to what they actually are.

Even a far-fetched image can work if it is appropriate. For example, war poet Wilfred Owen uses personification to describe dawn in the trenches:

> Dawn massing in the east her melancholy army
>
> Attacks once more in ranks on shivering ranks of grey ...

Even dawn, usually welcomed, is seen as an attacking army.

inappropriate imagery

What if the bell-ringers were described as 'a herd of mountain goats'? Goats kept in the mountains wear bells so they can easily be found, but this image would imply that the bell-ringers were wandering about, randomly ringing their bells, not working together to create music.

The simile at the start of 'Campanologists' is also surprising:

> It is as if they are milking the idea
>
> of angels, trying to draw down heaven

This daringly compares pulling the ropes to milking cows. But the image avoids being ridiculous by making it *the idea* of angels being milked, not angels themselves, and then explaining: 'trying to draw down heaven'.

paradoxical images

Some images work because they compare two things that are similar in at least one way, but very different in other ways. Look again at this section from 'Bell Ringers', which describes the bell-ringers feeling the rope ('the living cord') being pulled up in their hands as the bells swinging above.

> ... then feel the answering
>
> tug of grace that draws them up
>
> the living cord to a deep
>
> well above: the engine room
>
> of a heart that's hauling a whole
>
> invisible world down to make it
>
> matter

The metaphor calling the belfry (housing the bells) 'a deep well above' is paradoxical: the belfry is above the ringers, at the top of the tower, whereas a well is below ground level. Yet there is also a strong similarity: you let a bucket down a well on a rope and pull it up full of water; so a bell is like a bucket on a rope. Yet instead of water, the ringers get music that pours (like water) from the bells, and even something spiritual – 'a whole invisible world'. The image could also be called an **oxymoron**, combining apparently contradictory ideas.

Natural and unnatural imagery

Imagery can also work by comparing things from different worlds or **semantic fields**. The next two poems show how imagery can compare the natural world with the human.

Nile Kingfisher

First sight is black on white.
Quick wing-beats hammer,
businesslike,
tight-feathered with intent.

No wind-borne whimsy
but a short-haul scheduled flight,
clawed feet tucked
neat as an undercarriage
into feathers well-preened
and lightly oiled,
tail stub jutting out behind.

A to B straight in five seconds,
low over the water
drawn by the stab of a basalt beak,
jet-drilled and head-heavy.

> **Basalt** – smooth, jet black rock

Then perched on a felucca prow,
or plummeting air to water in a split,
dazzling dawn with spilt diamonds
and a silver minnow
shivering into death.

> **Felucca** – Egyptian sailing boat

Steve Eddy

k yourself

What words in stanza 1 link to the human world?

What metaphor describes the kingfisher in stanza 2?

How does line 1 of stanza 3 relate to the human world?

What are the 'spilt diamonds' in stanza 4?

Tench

The lake at dawn, a misted willow mirror.

Cast my line, shiver and wait,

the lipstick red tip of the float

an antenna to a clouded weed world.

First a flicker,

rippling like an infant's fingerprint

on a glass-topped table.

Then a plunge, rod bending, line taut.

Time stops. You break into thin air.

I reel you in:

tench, your slime-smooth skin the dark olive

of the depths you were dragged from.

Steve Eddy

k yourself

What does the metaphor in line 1 describe?

How is the fishing float (that bobs down when a fish takes the bait) 'an antenna'?

What is the effect of the simile in stanza 2?

How does alliteration contribute to the sense of the final line?

Summary

- Metaphors speak of something as if it *is* something else.
- Similes compare one thing with another using 'like', 'as' or 'than'.
- Personification describes an abstract idea as if it were a person or a god.
- Imagery works by comparing things that are similar in at least one way, but different in others.

Sample analysis

'Nile Kingfisher' uses a metaphor to compare the kingfisher with a jet, emphasising its power, and its direct, purposeful flight. The image of 'a short-haul scheduled flight' describes it in terms of a routine aspect of the human technological world, because the bird is just going about its daily business. The metaphor of water drops as 'spilt diamonds', however, presents the bird as a wonder of nature.

Questions

QUICK TEST
1. What kind of image uses 'like', 'as' or 'than'?
2. What is personification?
3. How does Wilfred Owen personify dawn in 'Exposure'?
4. How does 'Nile Kingfisher' use imagery to compare things from different worlds?

EXAM PRACTICE
Write a paragraph analysing the impact of imagery in 'Tench'.

and bless us despite ourselves. Though none
but we can make amends, your whisperings speak
all lovelessness into oblivion.

Cover our traces as we stumble on:
fill up our tracks, keep tumbling full and thick –
fall snow and cover all the hurt we've done,
spread over lovelessness oblivion.

Matthew Barton

k yourself

What is the effect of the soft 'f' alliteration in stanza 2, and the phrase 'soft resolve' in stanza 3, combining sibilance and assonance?

What lines or phrases are repeated, or almost repeated, and what is the effect?

What is the effect of internal rhyme (also assonance) in the final stanza ('stumble', 'tumbling')?

How does the poet personify the snow, and what is the effect?

Rain

Rain, midnight rain, nothing but the wild rain
On this bleak hut, and solitude, and me
Remembering again that I shall die
And neither hear the rain nor give it thanks
For washing me cleaner than I have been
Since I was born into this solitude.
Blessed are the dead that the rain rains upon:
But here I pray that none whom once I loved
Is dying to-night or lying still awake

Solitary, listening to the rain,

Either in pain or thus in sympathy

Helpless among the living and the dead,

Like a cold water among broken reeds,

Myriads of broken reeds all still and stiff,

Like me who have no love which this wild rain

Has not dissolved except the love of death,

If love it be for what is perfect and

Cannot, the tempest tells me, disappoint.

Edward Thomas

Ask yourself

- What words are repeated, and to what effect?
- What is the effect of alliteration in 'still and stiff'?
- What is the effect of the simile 'Like a cold water among broken reeds'?
- What is the effect of the 'd' and 'p' alliteration in the final three lines?

Summary

Alliteration is the repetition of consonant sounds at the beginnings of words or stressed syllables.

Assonance is the repetition of vowel sounds; it includes rhyme.

Onomatopoeia is the use of words that sound like their meaning.

Repetition of whole words or phrases can also be used for effect.

Sample analysis

'Fall Snow' uses alliteration and assonance to create a sense of the snow healing the emotional pain that people have caused. For example, the gentle 'l' and 'v' alliteration of 'Overlay the ache/ of lovelessness with your oblivion' contrasts with the harshness of 'ache'. The harmonising effect of assonance is found in 'soft resolve', though the phrase itself is an oxymoron, expressing the need to commit to kindness. The poem also repeats lines in an almost hypnotic way, while the repetitive rhyme scheme and enjambment, as in 'done/ to one another', accentuate the sense of healing.

Questions

QUICK TEST

. Which words show alliteration in 'kneel down from the night and cloak/ our lovelessness ...'?

. What effects can alliteration have?

. What sound effect is rhyme based on?

. Of which sound effect are 'fizz' and 'rumble' examples?

EXAM PRACTICE

Write a paragraph analysing the use of sound and repetition in 'Rain'.

The comparison question

How the two poems will be connected

The second exam question will give you a second poem to read and ask a question like th

> In both 'Piano' and 'Long Ago' the speakers describe childhood memories. What are the similarities and/or differences between the ways the poets present these memories?

The second poem will be more similar to the first in subject and themes than in form or style. For example, you could be given two poems about childhood memories, but not tw sonnets on unrelated subjects.

Focusing on the question

The focus of the two separate questions will probably overlap. For example, if the first poem was 'A Small Girl Swinging' (page 12), the first question might be:

> In 'A Small Girl Swinging', how does the poet present childhood experiences?

If the second poem was 'Piano' (pages 37–38), the comparison question might be:

> In both 'A Small Girl Swinging' and 'Piano' the speakers describe views of childhood. What are the similarities and/or differences between the ways the poets present the views?

Despite the overlap, it is important to focus on the exact question. Do not just compare random aspects of both poems.

'The ways the poets present ...'

The all-important phrase is 'the ways the poets present ...'. This refers to the aspects of voice, form and language summarised in the first section of this guide. You will not get many marks for this question without analysing techniques. So, which of the partial responses below do you think is better?

Response 1

'A Small Girl Swinging' describes childhood as a time of fear and insecurity, though mixed with some excitement. It also comments on the child's need of the absent mother. 'Piano', on the other hand, presents childhood as a time of happiness and security, with the child's intimate relationship with the mother ir the family home.

---

epare to compare

ad both unseen poems and questions before beginning to write about the first poem. s will give you a perspective on the first poem. In addition, reading both will allow you notice features in the first poem that will be relevant in the second question.

e comparison question carries only 8 marks, so spend about 12 minutes on it. Prepare annotating the first poem to answer the question. It may be helpful to circle or colour-de the relevant annotations you have already made. Then annotate features to compare the second poem. Aim to compare four or five similarities and differences – though you ld note more and then choose.

nnotation for comparison

ead 'Piano', and then a new poem, 'Long Ago', with similar themes. Both have been notated for this exam question:

ooth 'Piano' and 'Long Ago' the speakers describe the effects of memory. What are the ilarities and/or differences between the ways the poets present this theme?

iano

oftly, in the dusk, a woman is singing to me;

aking me back down the vista of years, till I see ← *Present tense; steady rhythm of memory dragging him.*

. child sitting under the piano, in the boom of ← *Pictures himself in detached way.*
    the tingling strings

nd pressing the small, poised feet of a mother
    who smiles as she sings.

n spite of myself, the insidious mastery of song

etrays me back, till the heart of me weeps ← *Mixed feelings – as if memory tricks him.*
    to belong

o the old Sunday evenings at home, with winter
    outside

And hymns in the cosy parlour, the tinkling piano
    our guide.

So now it is vain for the singer to burst
    into clamour

With the great black piano appassionato.
    The glamour

Of childish days is upon me, my manhood is cast

Down in the flood of remembrance, I weep like
    a child for the past.

Nostalgic, homely language.

Attraction – but false?

Climax: swept away

Long Ago

In a house I visited when I was young

I looked in through a partly opened door.

An old man sang 'Long Ago and Far Away'

To a rocking-horse, a friend's grandfather

Whose first-born son was lost at sea

Half-a-century before

In a ship whose name I have forgotten.

Image of partial nature of memory.

Sad detail – lost son's toy.

Whenever that sad song is played or sung

I'm in that house again, by that same door.

A woman tugs my sleeve. 'Come away,'

She says. 'Leave him alone.'

He sings, but he's no longer there.

The rocking-horse is rocking like the sea.

Ocean is everywhere

And the room is wind and rain.

Power of music.

Woman's anonymity; 'tugs', like memory.

Moving, haunting simile.

Emotion linked to water.

Douglas Dunn

sk yourself how both poems

use the senses

use symbolic objects

describe the power of music

use tenses

use water metaphorically.

Summary

- The second poem will be similar in subject and/or theme to the first.
- Focus on the exact question.
- 'The ways the poets present ...' refers to methods.
- Spend about 12 minutes on the comparison.

Sample analysis

n both poems, music triggers emotionally evocative memories. In 'Piano', the past is
seen visually as a returning 'vista', the steady rhythm reflecting its unfolding. In the
detached picture of 'a child', the third person phrasing shows the speaker's loss of his
childhood self. In 'Long Ago' there is more emphasis on the loss of the child who owned
the rocking horse, which, like both pianos in 'Piano', symbolises loss. Both poems,
however, use images of water for emotion: the 'flood' of remembrance in 'Piano' and
the ocean-filled room in 'Long Ago'.

Questions

QUICK TEST

1. What does 'the ways the poets present ...' refer to?
2. What should you focus on in answering the comparison question?
3. What key features do 'Piano' and 'Long Ago' share?
4. What is the key difference in the focus of the two poems?

EXAM PRACTICE

Write a plan for a comparison of how 'A Small Girl Swinging' and 'Long Ago' present
memories of the past and their emotional effect.

Writing a Comparison

There are two main methods of comparison, differing in how they approach similarities and differences. With either method you need to ensure that you write about both poem

For example, look again at the question used in the previous section:

> In both 'Piano' and 'Long Ago' the speakers describe the effects of memory. What are the similarities and/or differences between the ways the poets present this theme?

Despite the question typically using the phrase 'and/or differences', it is highly likely that there will be similarities *and* differences. The question will probably point out a basic similarity, so you might begin by extending this. For the question above, you could begin by writing:

> *In both poems music unlocks memories in the speaker that have powerful emotional effects.*

Which method to use?

You could get full marks using either method, but your comparison may be more fluent if you use the second method. On the other hand, the first is simpler. Try both and see which works better for you.

Comparison method 1

For this method, assuming you can find both similarities and differences, you then write one or more paragraphs about the similarities, then one or more paragraphs about the differences. You would need to make it clear at which point you were switching. You might, for example, begin a new paragraph with one of these phrases:

- 'On the other hand, ...'
- 'Despite these similarities, ...'
- 'Having said that, ...
- 'There are, however, significant differences ...'.

Ideally, finish with a further short paragraph summing up your comparison. Try not to simply repeat the earlier paragraphs.

Comparison method 2

This method involves comparing one or more aspects of both poems within a paragraph, then moving on to one or more different aspects of both poems in the next paragraph. Here is a plan for the question on 'Piano' and 'Long Ago' in the previous section:

Similar: music evokes memory and returns speaker to pictured childhood scene; also in sensory nature of memory and language: in 'Piano', visual metaphor 'vista', onomatopoeia of 'tingling' and 'tinkling'; touch of mother's feet. **Different:** 'Long Ago' focuses on sight ('partly opened door'), rocking-horse, touch ('tugs') and woman's voice. Only sense of music is 'sad song'.

Similar: memory evokes emotion. **Different**: Lawrence explicit about feelings ('my manhood is cast down ...'). Dunn implies he is haunted by memory: 'He sings, but he's no longer there.'

Similar: strong water imagery: 'Piano' has 'flood of remembrance'; 'Long Ago' rocking-horse still rocking, and 'Ocean is everywhere'. **Different**: 'Piano' more about speaker's personal loss; 'Long Ago' more about dead son, and general sadness of loss.

The language of comparison

Using method 1, you definitely need to use **link words** or phrases, with the correct punctuation, when you switch from similarities to differences. For method 2, however, it is helpful to use these whenever you make a comparison. Some additional link words and phrases are:

- whereas
- however
- moreover
- by contrast/comparison
- although.

Here is the first point in the plan above expanded, using links words and phrases (underlined):

The poems are <u>similar in that, in both,</u> music evokes memories that return the speaker to a pictured moment in childhood. <u>In addition,</u> the language of both expresses the sensory nature of memory. <u>However,</u> they use the senses in different ways. In 'Piano', 'vista' is visual, <u>but</u> the main focus is on sound, with the onomatopoeia of 'tingling' and 'tinkling', <u>whereas</u> 'Long Ago' focuses on the partial nature of memory, with the rocking-horse glimpsed through a 'partly opened door', on touch ('tugs') and the woman's words. <u>Moreover, while</u> 'Piano' gives a strong sense of both pieces of piano music, 'Long Ago' <u>merely</u> refers to the 'sad song'.

Comparing different aspects

Comparing narrative and structure

Ask yourself:

- Does each poem tell a story?
- If so, is it the story of an event?
- Does the story make a point?
- Does the structure follow the narrative?

For example, comparing 'Piano' and 'Long Ago', you could write:

> 'Piano' is in the present tense, and begins in the present moment, in which the speaker is listening to a concert that makes him remember himself as a child listening to his mother play piano. By contrast, 'Long Ago' is in the past tense and initially focuses on the past, its first stanza describing a moment when the speaker saw and heard an old man singing to a rocking-horse. In stanza 2 the poem shifts time frame, explaining how the song always takes him back to that moment. However, both poems end with similarly emotional imagery, 'Piano' with the speaker carried on the 'flood' of memory, and 'Long Ago' with the speaker haunted by the horse 'rocking like the sea'.

Comparing voice, viewpoint, tone and mood

Ask yourself:

- Is each poem in the first, second or third person?
- Is it written from a particular perspective (e.g. a persona)?
- What is the tone – for example, conversational, passionate?
- What mood is created?

For 'Piano' and 'Long Ago', you could write:

> 'Piano' is in the first person, the speaker frankly confessing the emotional effect of a concert on him, although he describes himself as 'a child', showing his detachment from that state. 'Long Ago', is also first person, but is far more conversational in tone. Whereas 'Piano' speaks nostalgically of the 'cosy parlour' of the speaker's childhood and confesses to weeping 'like a child for the past', the language of 'Long Ago' is understated, as in 'a ship whose name I have forgotten.' In 'Piano' the emotion is explicit; in 'Long Ago' it is quietly implied in the sea imagery of the last two lines.

Comparing form

Ask yourself:

- Does each poem have a metre or rhyme scheme?
- If so, what is the effect?
- How is each poem divided into stanzas?

You could write:

> The powerful emotional experience of 'Piano' is contained by the regular aabb rhyme scheme and the lines of roughly equal length. In addition, it is structured by stanzas, the first describing the memory being evoked, the second describing how the music 'betrays' the speaker emotionally, and the third dismissing the 'clamour' of the concert. Stanza division also features in 'Long Ago'. Stanza 1 describes a childhood moment in a matter-of-fact way, while stanza 2 describes how the song always returns the speaker to that moment. It has no third stanza, but the final two lines bring an emotional climax through water imagery, though in a quieter way than in 'Piano'.

Comparing language

Ask yourself:

- Can you compare word choices?
- What is the effect of any imagery?
- Are there noticeable sound effects, such as alliteration?

You could write:

> 'Piano' is dominated by sound, both in what it describes and how it does it. The vocalist sings 'softly in the dusk', the sibilance creating atmosphere. Lawrence uses onomatopoeia in 'boom of the tingling strings', and alliteration to suggest emotion creeping up on the listener in 'insidious mastery of song'. **Plosive** syllables burst dramatically in 'great black piano appassionato'. 'Long Ago' is much less dramatic, its iambic pentameter closer to ordinary speech, as in 'I'm in that house again, by that same door.' However, its repetition of 'rocking' in the second stanza, in another iambic line, creates a sense of waves on which the ghostly rocking-horse rocks.

Summary

- Choose whether to write about similarities first, then differences, or to write about them both within one paragraph at a time on each aspect.
- Use linking words and phrases to signpost points of comparison.
- Compare narrative, structure and form.
- Compare word choices and language.

Sample analysis

Imagery is used in a restrained way in both poems. In 'Piano' the poet sees the past as a landscape – a 'vista', and implies a personification of song in its 'insidious mastery' of his emotions, but its main image is the metaphorical 'flood of remembrance'. 'Long Ago' is dominated by the symbol of the dead son's rocking-horse, which rocks 'like the sea' in which he was lost. Both poems reach their climax in imagery relating water to emotion.

Questions

QUICK TEST
1. Which method of comparison is more likely to help you compare fluently?
2. What is the purpose of link words and phrases?
3. How do the stanzas relate to structure in 'Long Ago'?
4. How do 'Piano' and 'Long Ago' differ in their use of tense?

EXAM PRACTICE
Write a paragraph comparing the use of visual details in 'Piano' and 'Long Ago'.

u must be able to: understand how to approach the exam questions and meet the quirements of the mark scheme.

uick tips

Read both poems and questions to get an overview of your tasks and a perspective on each poem. Then reread the first poem and annotate it for answering the question.

Read the question carefully. It will ask you to comment on an aspect of the poem, not just to analyse the whole poem.

Think about how to interpret the question. For example, if the first poem was 'Long Ago' (page 56), and the question was 'How does the poet present memory?', you could include how the poem presents both the operation of memory and its effects.

The two unseen poetry questions combined carry one-third of the marks for Paper 2. So, spend about 45 minutes on them – about 33 minutes on the first poem, and 12 minutes on the comparison. Or think in terms of 30 minutes, 10 minutes, and 5 minutes to check.

Don't just identify poetic techniques: write about their *effects*.

Reread the question occasionally to keep yourself focused.

Write concisely, using brief quotations to support your points.

Focus on key details. Do not just summarise or generalise: it is better to say 'a lot about a little' rather than 'a little about a lot'.

Bear in mind the Assessment Objectives below.

sessment Objectives

st poem

1: Understand and respond to the poem (12 marks)

u should make a range of points in response to the question and the poem, supporting m with brief quotations or references, organising them logically, and writing in an propriately formal style.

Lower	Middle	Upper
A relevant response with some explanation and some supporting references from the poem.	A clear, explained response to the question; effective use of references to support explanation.	A critical, exploratory response to the question and the poem; well-chosen precise references to support interpretation(s).

AO2: Analyse effects of language, form and structure (12 marks)

You must analyse how word choices, language techniques, form and structure create meaning, using appropriate literary terminology (e.g. 'simile').

Lower	Middle	Upper
Identification of some poetic methods, with some comment on their effects, using some terminology.	A clear explanation of a range of poetic methods and their effects, using accurate terminology.	Insightful analysis of poetic methods and exploration of their effects, with a range of well-chosen and accurate terminology.

Comparison question

This question does not assess AO1. AO2 is assessed as for the main question, except that you will need to make comparisons and will not be expected to go into so much detail.

Lower	Middle	Upper
Some links between poets' use of language, structure or form and their effects on the reader.	A thoughtful comparison of poets' use of language, and/or structure, and/or form, and their effects; terminology used effectively to support analysis.	An exploratory and convincing comparison of poets' use of language, structure and form, and their effects; well-chosen terminology used effectively.

Read the two annotated poems below, and then the question on the first poem and annotated Grade 5 response.

Night Ferry

And our idea of hell is the night ferry. ◄———— Colloquial phrase includes reader; ferry symbolic?

A deep slow swell, the purser in his booth, ◄———— Rhythm imitates sea, slowed by alliteration.

A thumping head no aspirin can soothe

And two or three lads quietly getting merry. ◄———— Colloquial, emphasising normality; 'merry' contrasts with bleak mood.

It's normal, that is all, the bottom line

Of nightmare, meaning nothing, emptiness ◄———— 'N' alliteration negative.

Which finds us though we leave it no address ◄———— Personification

And leaves a pain that art cannot refine.

It's almost three o'clock. The vessel rolls: ◄———— Anchors to moment and ferry.

We draw our coats about us. The idea ◄———— Defence against elements.

Of sea enters our minds and washes clear

The bodies by their sinks and toilet bowls. ◄———— Upbeat ending; overcomes sordidness of sea-sickness.

George Szirtes

House on a Cliff

Indoors the tang of a tiny oil lamp. Outdoors ◄———— Alternates – in/out.

The winking signal on the waste of sea. ◄———— Alliteration.

Indoors the sound of the wind. Outdoors the
    wind.

Indoors the locked heart and the lost key.

Outdoors the chill, the void, the siren. Indoors ◄———— Cold, emptiness, danger?

The strong man pained to find his red blood cools,

While the blind clock grows louder, faster.
    Outdoors

— Significance of time.

The silent moon, the garrulous tides she rules.

— Opposites; night-time.

Indoors ancestral curse-cum-blessing. Outdoors
The empty bowl of heaven, the empty deep.
Indoors a purposeful man who talks at cross
Purposes, to himself, in a broken sleep.

— Night; metaphor emptiness.

Louis MacNeice

In 'Night Ferry', how does the poet present the experience of the ferry crossing? [24 mark

The speaker describes the ferry crossing as mostly horrible ('hell'). This is partly because of the effects of the sea.[1] There is a 'deep slow swell', which gives a feeling of the deep sea slowly rolling, and this gives the speaker 'a thumping head' that cannot be cured by aspirin, and makes other passengers throw up into 'sinks and toilet bowls'.[2] However, the purser seems to be all right, because he is in a booth, like the 'lads quietly getting merry'. This means they are able to get through the gloomy night by getting drunk at the bar. The word 'merry', which is happy, cheerful and informal, contrasts with the hell that the speaker feels.[3]

In the second verse the poet explores what the experience of the ferry crossing means, or why it is so awful. He uses quite ordinary language, 'It's normal, that is all', to say how ordinary the experience is, even though it is a 'nightmare'.[4] This seems to show a pessimistic view, as if life is a 'nightmare, meaning nothing, emptiness'. Perhaps being on the ferry in the middle of the night makes him feel negative about everything.[5]

1. Simple but effective comment on what poem is about, focusing on the question. AO1

2. Shows basic understanding, but too little analysis of words, and style sometimes too informal ('throw up'). AO1, AO2

3. Thoughtful analysis of effect of poet's word choice. AO2

4. Some attempt to analyse language. AO2

5. Attempts interpretation, but needs more evidence. AO2

The poet uses personification in the second verse. Emptiness is like a letter, or a postal worker, that finds the speaker even though he has left 'no address'. This makes it sound like this feeling of emptiness' cannot be avoided. It will get you even on a ferry at sea, when you are not at home.[6]

6. Accurate use of term, with thoughtful analysis – though 'it will get you' is too informal. AO2

The final verse switches to telling a sort of story. It brings the reader into the present moment by telling us the time in a short, simple sentence.[7] The ship rolling at that particular moment also gives a clear sense of the time, making us feel as if we were there.[8] The poet also appeals to the senses in 'We draw our coats about us.' This makes it clear that it is cold – he must be outside on the deck looking out at the sea. The use of the pronoun 'us' includes the reader, though maybe he is with a friend.[9]

7. Hints at narrative and begins to comment on effect of sentence form. AO2

8. Basic but effective comment on effect. AO2

9. Explores meaning, using technical term. AO2

The final sentence gives a twist.[10] At first it seems like the idea of sea is making people throw up, but maybe it is more that thinking about the sea out there actually stops him thinking about all that. In this way the poem has a kind of happy ending, despite the experience being generally unpleasant.[11]

10. Effective topic sentence. AO1

11. Explores meaning, providing competent conclusion that refers back to question. AO1, AO2

Questions

EXAM PRACTICE

Choose one or two paragraphs from this essay. Read them through a few times, then rewrite and improve them. You could:

- Change wording and sentence types to make the style more fluent and sophisticated.
- Use better quotations and ensure that they are embedded in sentences.
- Provide a more detailed or more insightful analysis.
- Use more subject terminology.

Grade 7+ Response

In 'Night Ferry', how does the poet present the experience of the ferry crossing? [24 mark

The poem describes a grim night ferry crossing that must be endured until the ferry docks. Its rhyme scheme and iambic pentameter give the experience form and make it bearable. The three stanzas structure it into a description of the crossing, an exploration of its meaning, and a final epiphany.[1]

1. Effective introduction commenting on form and structure. AO1, AO2

The opening 'And', is unsettling as if it is a continuation. The use of 'our' also creates uncertainty: it could refer to the speaker and a companion, or people generally, including the reader. 'Our idea of hell' is a colloquial exaggeration but it could also be taken literally, as if the crossing is a metaphor for hell.[2]

2. Close, insightful focus on effects of language choices. AO2

After the opening statement, the speaker justifies it. The dragging non-iambic rhythm of 'deep slow swell' combines with alliteration to create an unsettling sense of the rolling sea causing the speaker's headache, described as 'thumping', as if the sufferer is repeatedly hit, and possibly echoing the engine noise.[3] It also makes other passengers sick into 'sinks and toilet bowls'. Even 'lads quietly getting merry' at the bar is bleak. The colloquial language makes it sound commonplace, and 'merry' seems weak when contrasted with the 'hell' they are trying to keep at bay.[4] There being only 'two or three' of them also paints a sad picture. The only other passengers mentioned are just sea-sick 'bodies'.

3. Insightful analysis of language; judicious use of terminology. AO2

4. Precise analysis of word choice. AO2

In stanza 2, banal language expresses the
ordinariness of the experience: 'It's normal,
that is all'. It is as if the 'bottom line' of human
existence is a 'nightmare'. The alliteration of
'normal', 'nightmare' and 'nothing' links these words
in negativity.[5] 'Emptiness' is personified as the
deliverer of an unwanted parcel that reaches us
even with no address, implying that this feeling
is unavoidable.[6] Even the poet's own 'art' cannot
improve it.

Stanza 3 switches to a narrative, the short
simple sentence announcing the time taking us
into the poem's present moment, and emphasising
how time drags on the crossing.[7] 'The vessel rolls'
also brings the physical experience to life, aided
by the sense of cold in 'draw our coats about us':
passengers are doing their best to find comfort.[8]
It also places the speaker on deck, along with 'us'.

In the final sentence, however,[9] the inspirational
idea of 'sea' replaces the sordid discomfort of sea-
sickness. It is as if the speaker has been seized by
the sea's physical presence, and this has lifted 'us'
out of the 'nightmare' of 'emptiness' explored in
stanza 2.[10]

The poem takes an experience that has to be
endured, and that is a metaphor for human
suffering, and finally transcends it through a
direct experience of nature.[11]

5. Effective interpretation of word choice, with terminology. AO2

6. Insightful and fluent analysis of correctly named technique. AO2

7. Awareness of structure and use of sentence types. AO2

8. Insightful interpretation. AO2

9. Effective use of link word. AO1

10. Insightful interpretation, supported by well-chosen embedded quotations. AO1, AO2

11. Effective conclusion summing up poem's impact without repetition. AO1, AO2

Questions

EXAM PRACTICE
Cover up the annotations, then reread the essay and try to list five of its most effective
features. You could write notes on the actual essay – in pencil if you prefer.

Grade 5 Comparison

Both 'Night Ferry' and 'House on a Cliff' show human beings in a state of struggle, influenced by the elements. What are the similarities and/or differences between the way the poets describe their feelings? [8 marks]

Both poems are about individuals at night influenced by the sea, struggling with their feelings.[1] 'Night Ferry' is clearer. The speaker hates the ferry crossing and it makes him feel empty. In 'House on a Cliff' there is a similar sense of bleakness, but no clear cause. The 'tiny oil lamp' creates a gloomy picture, with the 'waste of sea', the wind, and the man's 'locked heart'. Like the speaker of 'Night Ferry', he is unhappy ('pained'), but we don't know why, and there is less sense of his identity.[2]

In both poems it is cold. In 'Night Ferry' we know this from people drawing their coats around them, but 'House on a Cliff' is more straightforward: 'chill'. In 'Night Ferry' the 'nothing, emptiness' is the speaker's response to the crossing. In 'House on a Cliff' it is the emptiness of the night outside the house, and beyond the cliff, as well as the 'empty bowl' of the sky.[3]

Each poem is three verses, but they are structured differently. 'Night Ferry' moves from description, to discussion, to now, on deck. 'House on a Cliff', on the other hand, switches between indoors and outdoors throughout.[4] 'Night Ferry' contrasts the indoors of the bar, and the booth, and the outdoors of the deck, but it seems more natural. In 'House on a Cliff' the contrast is more dramatic and artificial.[5]

1. Effective introductory sentence.

2. Good comparative points, but explanation and evidence needed.

3. Clear comparison, though could explore imagery.

4. Effective comparison of form.

5. Interesting point but needs explanation and evidence.

There are other opposites all through 'House on a Cliff', like 'silent moon, the garrulous [talkative] tides' and 'curse' versus 'blessing'. Both poems use personification, 'Night Ferry' for the emptiness, and 'House on a Cliff' for the moon. In both cases this gives an image of power.[6]

> 6. Simple but effective analysis of technique's effect, using technical term.

Questions

EXAM PRACTICE

Choose one or two paragraphs from this essay. Read them through a few times, then rewrite and improve them. You could:

- Change wording and sentence types to make the style more fluent.
- Use link words to add fluency.
- Provide a more insightful analysis.
- Use more subject terminology.

Grade 7+ Comparison

Both 'Night Ferry' and 'House on a Cliff' show human beings in a state of struggle, influenced by the elements. What are the similarities and/or differences between the wa the poets describe their feelings? [8 marks]

Both poems depict individuals at night influenced by the elements, struggling with negative feelings. However, in 'Night Ferry' a narrator tries to explain why the crossing is difficult, universalising it with the pronoun 'us'. 'House on a Cliff' conveys a similar bleakness, but the reader is given a series of impressions formulaically introduced only by the alternating 'Indoors' and 'Outdoors'.[1]

1. Highly effective introduction to key similarities and differences.

Both characters are unhappy, but in 'Night Ferry' this is 'normal', whereas in 'House on a Cliff' the man's 'locked heart' suggests that he cannot love. In addition, in 'Night Ferry' the speaker's experience 'leaves a pain', whereas in 'House on a Cliff' the man is also 'pained' but more enigmatic.[2] *Even the personified moon and talkative tides make him seem more isolated.*[3]

2. Excellent comparison of similar language and its effects.

3. Very effective analysis of technique, using correct term.

In 'Night Ferry' passengers are joined in a shared seeking of comfort, in the bar and on deck. In 'House on a Cliff', by contrast, the man is alone, surrounded by 'the chill, the void, the siren'. All are comfortless, and the siren suggests danger.[4]

4. Insightful comparison and interpretation.

Structurally,[5] *'Night Ferry' moves from description, to exploration, to present moment narrative, while 'House on a Cliff' alternates between indoors and outdoors throughout.*

5. Good use of adverb to flag up what paragraph is about.

'Night Ferry' compares indoors and on-deck, but this flows as part of the narrative. 'House on a Cliff' dramatically juxtaposes the two worlds, beginning and ending indoors.[6] This gives a sense of the man being stuck, whereas the speaker in 'Night Ferry' is finally relieved by the thought of the sea.[7]

The narrative of 'Night Ferry' is reflected in its conversational language, its only image being the personification in stanza 2. 'House on a Cliff' is self-consciously poetic: alliteration and assonance strengthen the metaphor of the 'locked heart and the lost key', and the 'empty bowl' metaphor suggests an emotional starvation linked to the man's isolation.[8]

> 6. Effective and succinct observation.

> 7. Insightful interpretation.

> 8. Excellent comparison of language, using appropriate terminology.

Questions

EXAM PRACTICE

Reread the Grade 5 and Grade 7+ comparison responses. Then write an examiner-style paragraph summarising why the Grade 7+ deserves the higher grade. Try to include four points, with examples where possible.

Consider:

- organisation
- fluency, including use of link words and phrases to signpost comparison
- level of analysis
- use of subject terminology.

1. In 'She Dwelt among the Untrodden Ways' (page 10), how does the poet present hi feelings about the girl?

2. In both 'She Dwelt among the Untrodden Ways' and 'A Small Girl Swinging' (page the speakers describe views of childhood. What are the similarities and/or differenc between the ways the poets present these views?

3. In 'Traffic' (page 14), how does the poet present his feelings about his situation?

4. In both 'Traffic' and 'A Cry from the Blue' (pages 15–16) the speakers describe experiences of time. What are the similarities and/or differences between the ways the poets present their experiences?

5. In both 'Traffic' and 'Night Ferry' (page 65) the speakers describe difficult journeys. What are the similarities and/or differences between the ways the poets present th experiences?

6. In 'The Thief of Love' (pages 20–21), how does the poet present love?

7. The speakers of both 'The Thief of Love' and 'Fall Snow' (pages 50–51) describe aspects of love. What are the similarities and/or differences between the ways the poets present attitudes to love?

8. In 'A Birthday' (pages 23–24), how does the poet present love?

9. In both 'A Birthday' and 'Fall Snow' the speakers describe aspects of love. What are the similarities and/or differences between the ways the poets present their feeling

10. In 'White Van Man' (page 25), how does the poet present the character and life of the man?

11. Both 'White Van Man' and 'An Irish Airman Foresees his Death' (page 19) present characters. What are the similarities and/or differences between the ways the poets present these characters?

12. In 'Being Dead' (pages 28–29), how does the poet present the character of the woman?

13. Both 'Being Dead' and 'White Van Man' present characters. What are the similaritie and/or differences between the ways the poets do this?

14. In 'The Voice' (pages 29–30), the poet presents memories of a loved one. How does present these memories and the feelings they arouse?

15. 'The Voice' and 'Piano' (page 36) both present memories. What are the similarities and/or differences between the ways the poets present their memories and feelings

16. In 'On the Grasshopper and Cricket' (page 38), the poet presents his experience of nature. How does he do this?

Both 'On the Grasshopper and Cricket' and 'A Birthday' (pages 23–24) present joyful experiences. What are the similarities and/or differences between the ways the poets present these experiences?

Both 'On the Grasshopper and Cricket' and 'Nile Kingfisher' (page 46) could be called nature poems. What are the similarities and/or differences between the ways the poets present nature?

In 'Bell Ringers' (page 41), how does the poet present the experience of bell-ringing?

Both 'Bell Ringers' and 'Campanologists' (page 42) describe bell-ringing. What are the similarities and/or differences between the ways the poets present their views of this activity?

In 'Fall Snow' (pages 50–51), how does the poet present the experience of snow?

Both 'Fall Snow' and 'Rain' (pages 51–52) describe weather. What are the similarities and/or differences between the ways the poets present their responses to weather?

Glossary

Alliteration – repetition of consonant (non-vowel) sounds at the beginnings of words or stressed syllables (e.g. 'carving a career, making his mark').

Ambiguity – a double meaning (adj. 'ambiguous').

Anapaest – a rhythmic **foot** of three syllables, two unstressed and one stressed.

Assonance – repetition of vowel sounds (e.g. fish, bit).

Ballad – narrative poem, often with a tragic ending, written in **ballad metre**.

Ballad metre – verse form consisting of **stanzas** of four lines each, in which lines 1 and 3 are in **tetrameter** (four **feet**), and lines 2 and 4 in **trimeter** (three **feet**). Lines 2 and 4 usually rhyme.

Blank verse – unrhymed (blank) **iambic pentameter**.

Connotation – association of a word with other things or ideas, e.g. fire with heat or passion.

Couplet – pair of lines, often rhyming.

Dactyl – a rhythmic **foot** of three syllables, one stressed and two unstressed.

Elegy – poem celebrating the life of someone who has died.

Enjambment – running the sense of a phrase on from one line to the next.

Epitaph – inscription on a gravestone, sometimes in verse form.

Foot – syllabic unit of rhythm, repeated to form a metre.

Form – poem's verse patterns and how it is divided into **stanzas**.

Iamb (adj. iambic) – a verse **foot** of one unstressed syllable followed by one stressed.

Iambic pentameter – metrical line of five **iambs**.

Iambic tetrameter – metrical line of four **iambs**.

Internal rhyme – rhyme within lines of verse rather than at their ends.

Irony – something seemingly inappropriate in a grimly comic way.

Limerick – comic poem of five **anapaestic** lines rhyming *aabba*.

Link words (connectors) – words or phrases signposting argument, such as 'however' or 'on the other hand'.

Litotes – understatement.

Metaphor – image speaking of something as it *is* something else.

Metre – poem's rhythmic pattern, including the types and numbers of **feet** it has in a line.

Mood – overall emotional effect of a poem or a significant part of it.

Narrative (noun and adj.) – telling a story.

Octave – first eight lines of a **Petrarchan sonnet**, which put forward an idea.

Onomatopoeia – use of words that sound like their meaning, e.g. 'fizz'.

Oxymoron – combination of apparently contradictory ideas, e.g. 'cold fire'.

Pentameter – line of verse with five **feet**, especially **iambic pentameter**.

Persona – narrator or speaker of a poem assuming a particular identity, e.g. 'An Irish Airman Foresees his Death'.

Personification – type of metaphor describing an abstract idea, such as love or time, as if it were a person or a god.

...rarchan sonnet – a poem of 14 lines, in ...ich the first eight (the **octave**) put forward ...idea, while the final six (the **sestet**) develop ...n a new direction, often bringing it to a ...olution.

...sive – consonant speech sound that seems ...explode, created by sudden release of air, ...in 'black piano appassionato'.

...n – play on a word with two meanings, ...'strain' meaning both effort and tune.

...atrain – four-line **stanza**.

...etorical question – question asked for effect ...her than expecting an answer.

...yme – sound effect produced by a repeated ...vel sound and consonant, but with a ...ferent consonant sound following it.

...yme scheme – pattern of **rhyme**; can be ...noted by letters, as in *abab*.

...mantic field – broad grouping of words ...ociated with a particular area of life, e.g. ...ence.

...stet – six lines ending a **Petrarchan sonnet**.

...akespearean sonnet – 14-line poem with a ...st or resolution in a final rhyming **couplet**.

Sibilance (adj. sibilant) – type of **alliteration** featuring hissing sounds, especially 's', but also 'sh' and 'z'.

Simile – image comparing one thing with another explicitly, using 'like', 'as' or 'than'.

Sonnet – 14-line poem; *see also* **Petrarchan sonnet**; **Shakespearean sonnet**.

Stanza – separate section of verse.

Symbol (adj. symbolic) – thing representing an idea or emotion, e.g. sword for conflict.

Tetrameter – line of four metrical **feet**.

Theme – idea explored in a poem, beyond its obvious subject, e.g. childhood innocence.

Tone – how the poet addresses the reader – for example, in a conversational tone, or a bitter tone.

Trimeter – line of three metrical **feet**.

Trochee (adj. trochaic) – metrical **foot** of two syllables, one stressed and one unstressed.

Voice – person or character whom we imagine speaking a poem, which may or may not simply be the poet speaking as himself or herself.

Answers

Pages 4–9: How to Approach a Poem

QUICK TEST

1. The subject is what it appears to be about; themes are the ideas it explores (e.g. love or conflict).

2. Metre

3. Simile

EXAM PRACTICE

The first stanza sets the scene for the speaker's time of 'blissful dreams' but does not yet reveal what she wishes she could see when awake. Alliteration connects and emphasises 'blissful' and 'bless'. Stanza 2 focuses on hearing, revealing that she desires contact with a lost loved one. The final stanza touches on the 'cold' reality, but gives a sense of completion and hope by returning to the 'bliss' and 'dreams' of the opening stanza.

Pages 10–13: What is it About? How Subject Relates to Theme

QUICK TEST

1. Swinging

2. Textual evidence, in the form of a short quotation or reference.

3. Possible themes: childhood, innocence, loss.

4. She seems to be uneasy, fearful, feeling abandoned because her mother is too far away to hear. Shadows suggest threat.

EXAM PRACTICE

The girl is 'very scared' from the start, and then full of menacing 'whisperings' of fears. This changes to excitement in the middle stanzas, in which her leaping heart could signify both exhilaration and nervousness. The repetition of 'fourth time' slows the poem down, as if she is relishing the memory. In the final two stanzas, however, a sense of threat returns and grows, with the girl left alone, feeling 'small', still swinging but abandoned, with shadows all around.

Pages 14–18: What is it About? Narrative Poems

QUICK TEST

1. (b) and (c)

2. Structure

3. It emphasises his car being stuck in traffic for what seems like a very long time.

EXAM PRACTICE

In the sudden silence after his lawnmower has stalled, the narrator has heard a sound that he cannot identify but which comes to represent something mysteriously significant. His personification of 'inanimate objects' being surprised seems to describe his own sudden experience of them as if he were absent himsel He seems disturbed by the 'portentous' nature the noise, unsettled, as if the world could colla without explanation, like the 'books that crash if pushed by an invisible hand.

Pages 19–22: Voice, Viewpoint, Tone and Mood

QUICK TEST

1. 'My countrymen Kiltartan's poor' shows tha the airman is an Irishman from a poor, rura background.

2. It is addressed to 'you', which presents a direct threat to the reader.

3. 'Love has no pride'

EXAM PRACTICE

The airman regards his death as his inevitable 'fate', and is unconcerned about when or whe it will happen: it will just be 'somewhere' in the vagueness of 'above the clouds'. His simple language in 'Those that I fight ...' suggests tha he is, ironically for an airman, a down-to-earth character, who has no passion or patriotism. However, he is sensitive to the fact that the poor's condition will be unchanged by the war Nothing will 'bring them loss/ Or leave them happier'. He did not join up for conventional reasons, such as 'law' or 'duty'. Rather, he felt future was 'a waste of breath' and was moved an 'impulse' to fly.

Pages 23–27: Viewpoint, or Perspective

QUICK TEST

1. He, she, it

2. Stanza 1 describes the speaker's feelings of joy, using similes of nature. In stanza 2 she sees herself as elevated by happiness to the status of royalty, and orders all the trappin of that status. Stanza 2 is based on details c luxury, rather than on similes.

3. Present tense is likely to make it seem more immediate.

4. It makes him seem down-to-earth, a strong simple, straightforward character – like a shovel. The 'b' alliteration accentuates this.

EXAM PRACTICE

He is a down-to-earth, straightforward farmer, as suggested by the image of his beard. He likes women but prefers horses, and is like one

self – a 'cob', the simple rhyme with his name
phasising his simplicity. He is leather-coloured
n being sun-tanned by his outdoor life, but
:her also suggests toughness. The poet makes
a non-judgemental lover of 'most living
ngs'. His special love of trees fits his character,
ted in the countryside. His planting suggests
t he cared about future generations.

es 28–31: Tone and Mood

CK TEST

Tone is the poet's style of address, especially
relating to level of formality, but including,
for example, sad, angry, humorous and
cynical. Mood is the emotional effect of a
poem or part of it.

Strongly emotional poems.

Informal language, rhyme, formal language
used ironically, onomatopoeia.

There is a sudden change in the final stanza
to a dragging rhythm, exaggerated by
alliteration, suggesting an old man 'faltering
forward' uncertainly, or without hope or
enthusiasm.

AM PRACTICE

hough the poet is addressing a lost love, the
t two stanzas are buoyed up by the thought
t he can hear her voice. The strong, regular
tylic rhythm reflects this. In the second
nza he even imagines he can see her, with
visual detail of her gown raising the mood.
wever, the rhythm slows in the third stanza
h the awkward rhyme of 'listlessness' and
tlessness', and harsh reality is suggested by
apathetic breeze and the wet meadow, and
idea that the woman is 'dissolved'. However,
real change comes in the final stanza, with
Iragging rhythm, exaggerated by alliteration,
gesting an old man 'faltering forward'
ertainly, without hope or enthusiasm, and the
ails of the autumn leaves and north wind.

es 32–35: Forms and Structure

CK TEST

Iambic (one unstressed and stressed syllable).

A metre consisting of five units of syllables –
usually iambic (so, five pairs of syllables).

A repeated unit of rhythm, e.g. an iambic
foot is one pair of syllables.

If writing in a metre, they choose an
appropriate one, and vary it for effect.

AM PRACTICE

first four stanzas are in a regular iambic
thm, with the short lines of trimeter often

sounding childlike – as in 'My skirt flew off the
world.' Then 'The fourth time, Oh, the fourth
time' forces a break, with 'Oh' creating a sense
of longing for that happy time. However, the
change to a dragging dactylic rhythm in the fifth
stanza creates a change of mood, accentuated by
the two-syllable rhymes of ringing–swinging and
calling–falling. The effect is to make the mood
less childlike and more ominous.

Pages 36–39: Structure

QUICK TEST

1. A metre is often repeated with each new
   stanza.

2. It tells a story – its structure is narrative.

3. Present tense: emphasises how the present
   moment drags the speaker back to the past,
   which then overwhelms his experience of the
   present – the concert.

4. Octave (8 lines) and sestet (6 lines).

EXAM PRACTICE

The octave presents summer, embodied by the
grasshopper; the sestet presents winter, embodied
by the cricket. Together they confirm the power
of nature to endure through the changing
seasons, presented in the first line in each part in
slightly different form: 'never dead' and 'ceasing
never'. The hot sun dominates the octave, the
cold winter the sestet, but the cricket serves as
a reminder of summer in winter, connecting the
two creatures through the listener.

Pages 40–43: Language

QUICK TEST

1. Childlike, naïve.

2. It suggests that his memories are seductive –
   both attractive and unreliable.

3. Symbolism is the use of a material thing
   (as opposed to an idea) to represent an idea,
   e.g. a dove representing peace.

4. It implies that bell ringing is productive work,
   not just a pastime.

EXAM PRACTICE

The poet compares pulling the bell ropes to
'milking', which suggests that it is like a farmer
pulling on the udders of a cow. However, it also
suggests getting something nourishing and
pure by doing this, perhaps even the 'milk of
human kindness'. There is also a pun in 'strain',
referring both to effort and music. 'Raucous
tintinnabulation' is an interesting choice, the
adjective and onomatopoeic noun implying a noisy
clanging rather than beautiful music, reflecting
'complaints and grievances' rather than praise.

Pages 44–48: Imagery

QUICK TEST

1. A simile.
2. Using the image of a person or god to represent an idea, e.g. 'Old Father Time', or Cupid for love.
3. As the commander of an army.
4. It describes the bird in terms of a jet plane.

EXAM PRACTICE

The lake's stillness is captured in 'willow mirror': it reflects the trees overhanging it. The float being 'lipstick red' describes its bright colour and hints at its shape. Both this and 'antenna' suggest the human world incongruously entering the natural, the latter also suggesting, nonetheless, an invisible connection between the two. The 'fingerprint' simile carries on the idea of the lake's stillness, as well as suggesting the delicate, unsuspecting touch of the fish causing the ripple.

Pages 49–53: Sound Effects

QUICK TEST

1. 'kneel' and 'night'; by some definitions also 'lovelessness'.
2. It can connect the meanings of words, or contrast them. It can also create a sense of harmony.
3. Assonance. A rhyme is created by a repeated vowel sound and consonant, but with a different consonant sound following it. So, 'floor' and 'pour' rhyme because the vowel sounds and endings are the same.
4. Onomatopoeia

EXAM PRACTICE

The word 'rain' occurs seven times in the poem – three times in the first line, and again coupled with 'rains'. This emphasises the constancy of the rain, and the way it dominates the speaker's thoughts. His 'solitude' is also emphasised by repetition. Sounds shape meaning throughout the poem, such as the dead 'd' sounds of 'solitude', 'blessed' (pronounced as two syllables) and 'dead' itself. Another example is the alliteration and assonance in 'still and stiff', the repeated sound reflecting the identical form of the 'Myriads' of reeds.

Pages 54–57: Comparing Poems

QUICK TEST

1. The poetic methods used to create meaning in the poem.
2. The exact question (i.e. not just all aspects of both poems).
3. In both, music triggers emotionally evocative memories. Both use water imagery for emotion.

4. 'Piano' focuses on the speaker's loss of childhood happiness, 'Long Ago' on a childhood memory of someone else's loss.

EXAM PRACTICE

- Both focus on childhood memories, but SGS ('A Small Girl Swinging') covers memories numbered 1–4, then comes into present.
- SGS narrator may still be a child, suggested e.g. 'tummy jiggled'; LA ('Long Ago') narrate by adult looking back ('when I was young').
- SGS moves from past tense to threatening present tense; LA narrates incident in past tense, then moves into present to indicate song's effect.
- SGS ends on note of threat – absent mothe and 'shadows'; LA ends with image of overwhelming weather and ocean.

Pages 58–62: Writing a Comparison

QUICK TEST

1. Comparing similarities and differences for one aspect within one paragraph, then doi the same in subsequent paragraphs.
2. They show the reader how your argument progresses, making connections between ideas, highlighting your comparison.
3. The first stanza narrates the incident, using past tense; the second uses present tense to describe how the speaker is now affected b the song.
4. 'Piano' is all in the present tense; 'Long Ag shifts from past to present.

EXAM PRACTICE

'Piano' describes the unfolding memories recedin to the point of childhood as a 'vista', suggesting a landscape over which the speaker gazes. The only other strongly visual detail is the 'great blac piano', which suggests an unfavourable comparis between a full-size grand piano and a small upright one. 'Long Ago' is more visual, focusing on the memory of an old man and a rocking-hor glimpsed through 'a partly opened door'. The speaker associates the song with this visual mem

Pages 72–73: Grade 7+ Comparison

EXAM PRACTICE

The Grade 5 comparison makes some good point but lacks sufficient explanation and evidence, an could explore the effects of imagery. The Grade 7 comparison is more detailed, more insightful, an is more successful in analysing effects, especially of structure and imagery. It also uses more terminology, always accurately, and with an anal of effects, especially in the final paragraph.